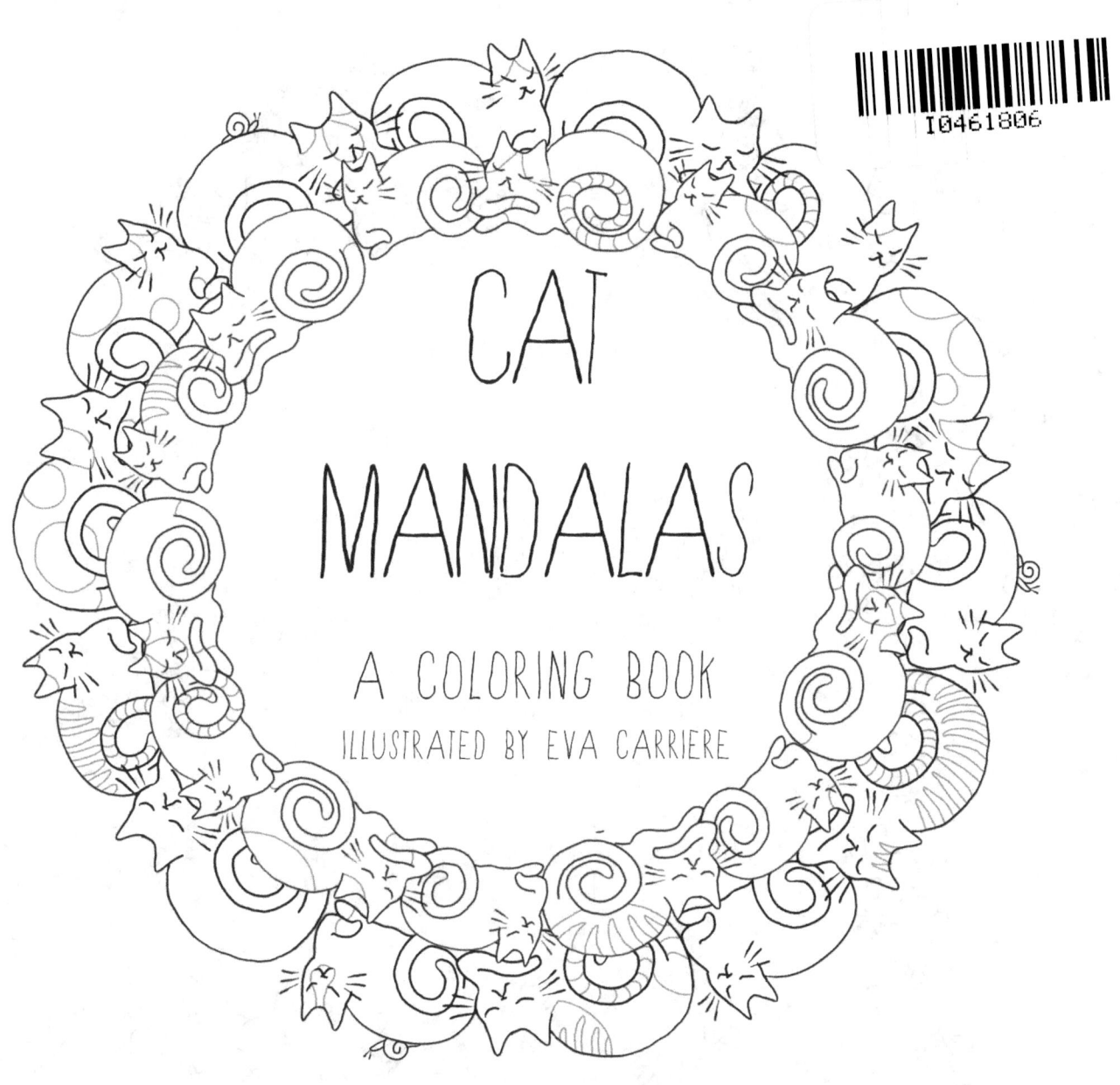

CAT
MANDALAS
A COLORING BOOK
ILLUSTRATED BY EVA CARRIERE

"THE SMALLEST FELINE
IS A MEOWSTERPIECE."
-LEONARDO PAW VINCI

QUIXOTE PRESS

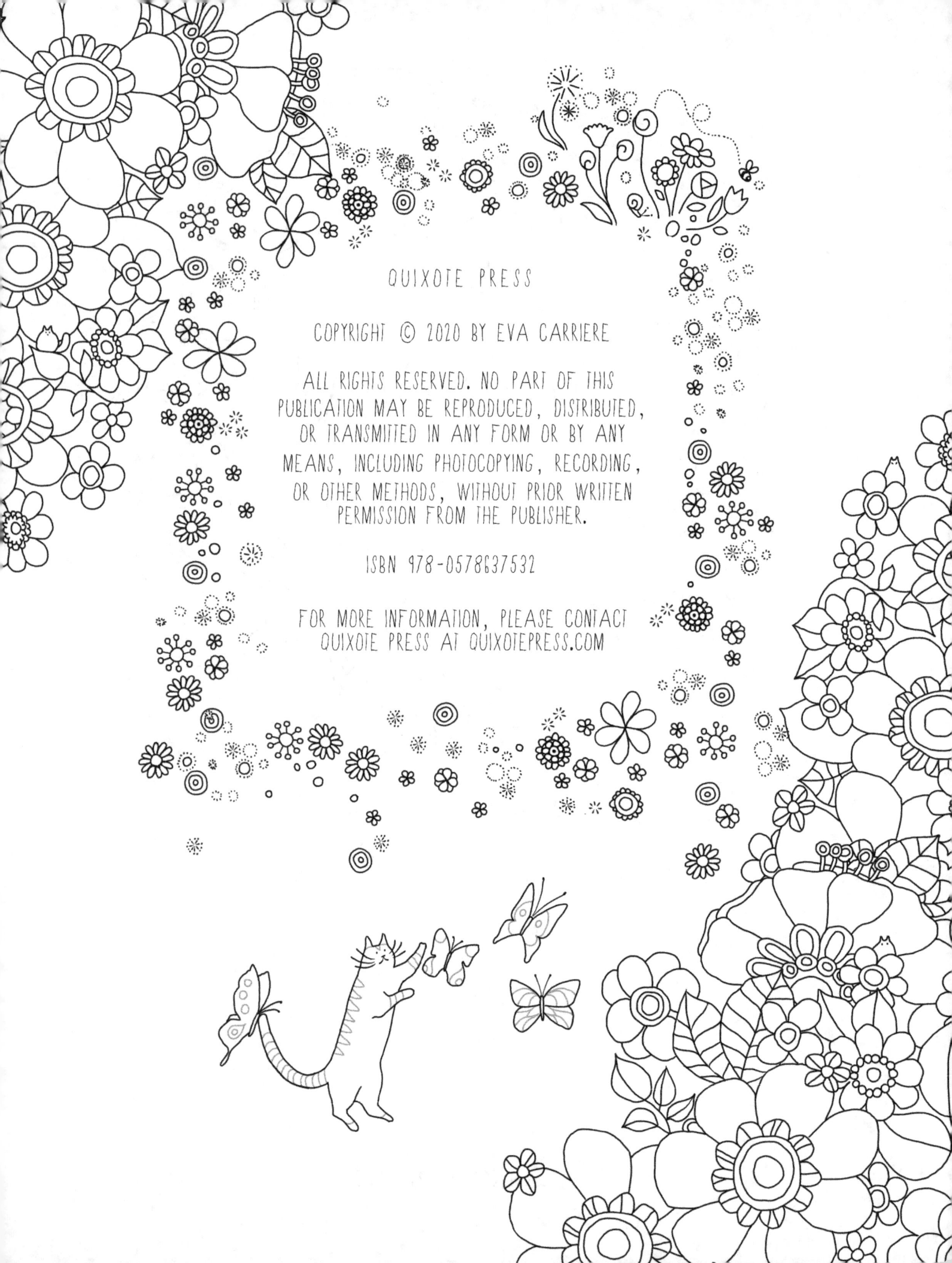

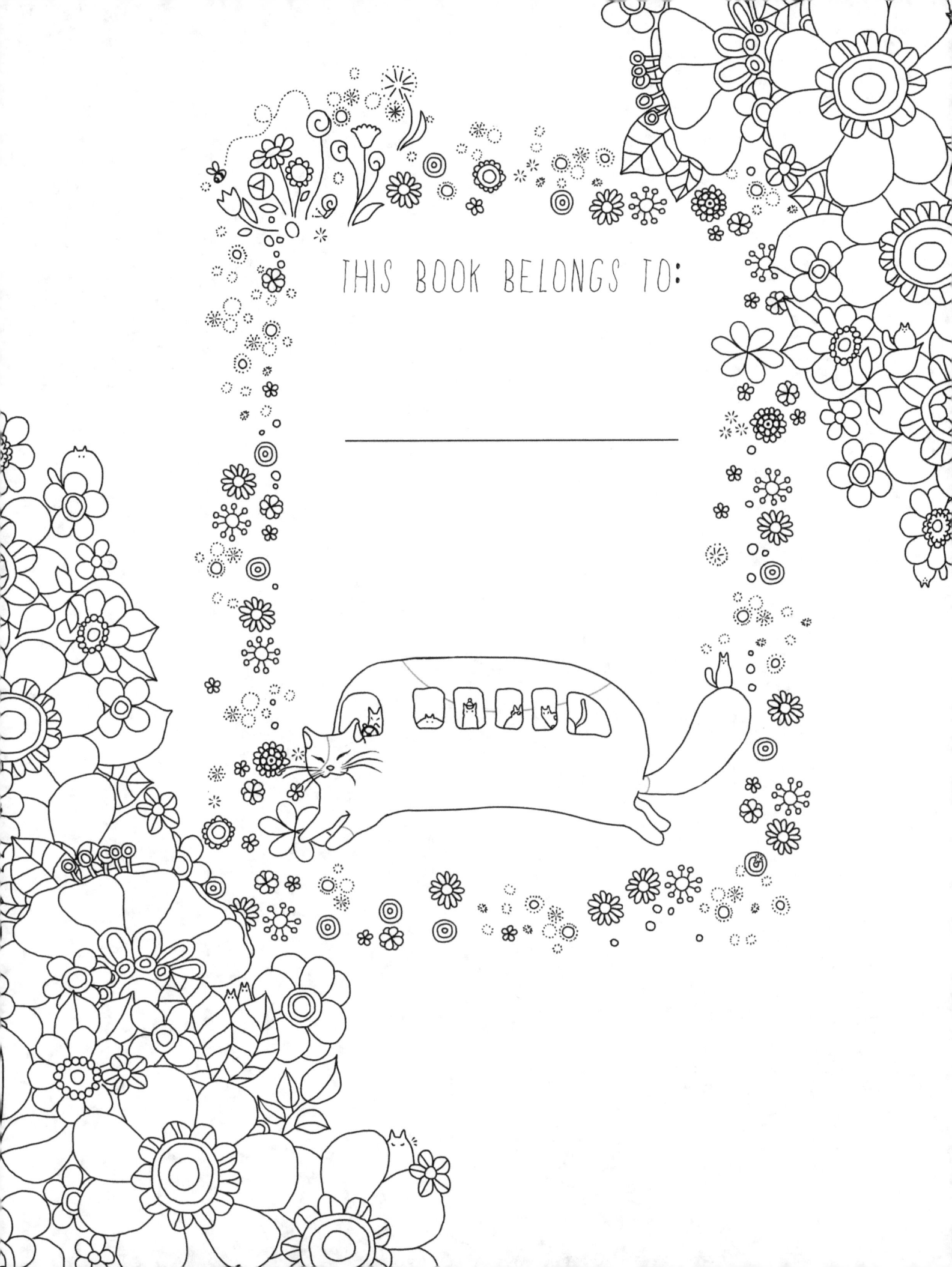

THIS BOOK BELONGS TO:

_____

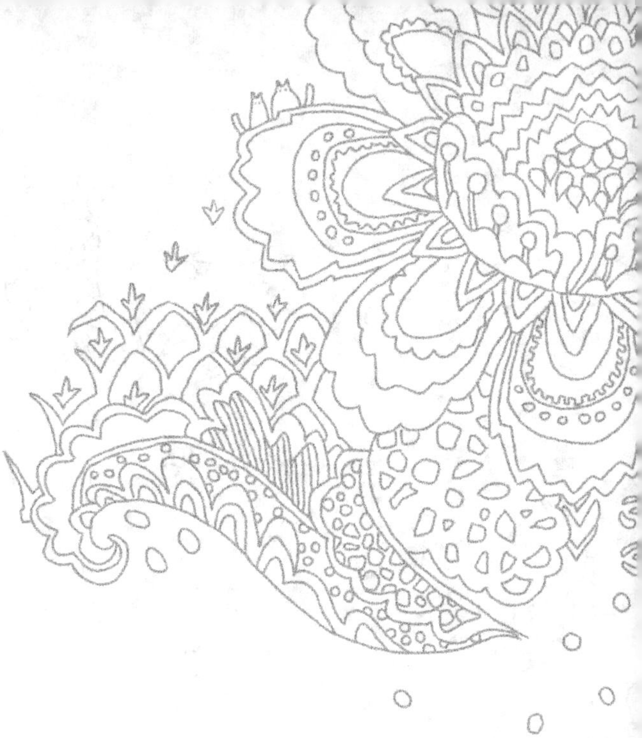

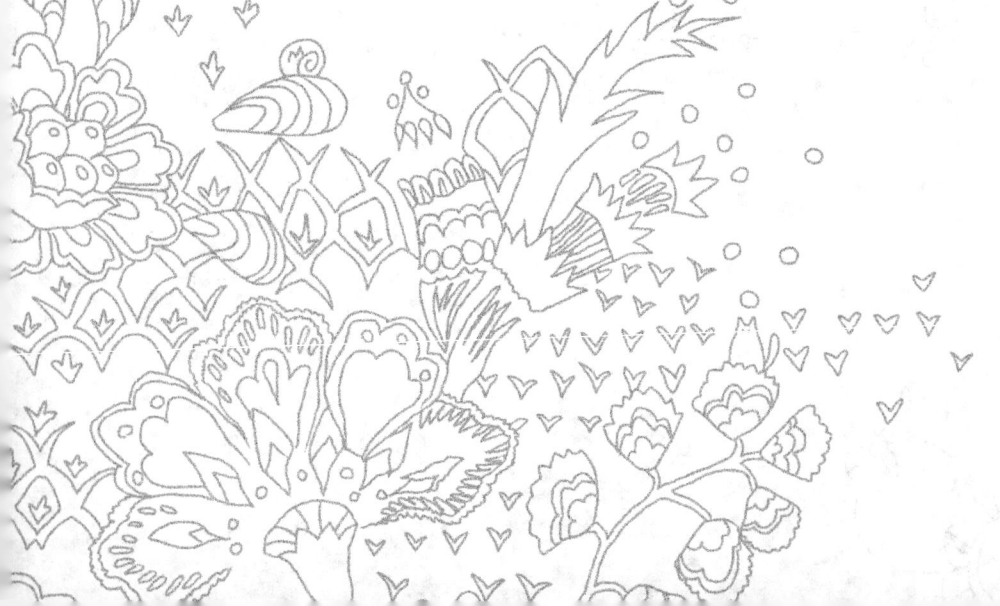

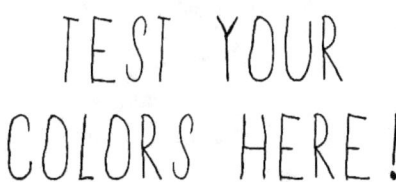

TEST YOUR
COLORS HERE!

COLORING TIP: TO PREVENT BLEED-THROUGH WHEN USING MARKERS, BE SURE TO HAVE A SHEET OF SCRAP PAPER STUCK BEHIND THE PAGE YOU'RE COLORING.

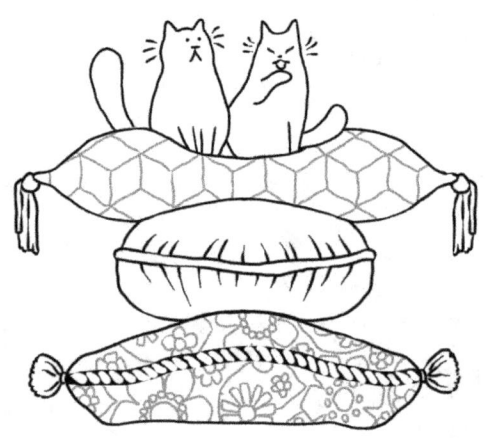

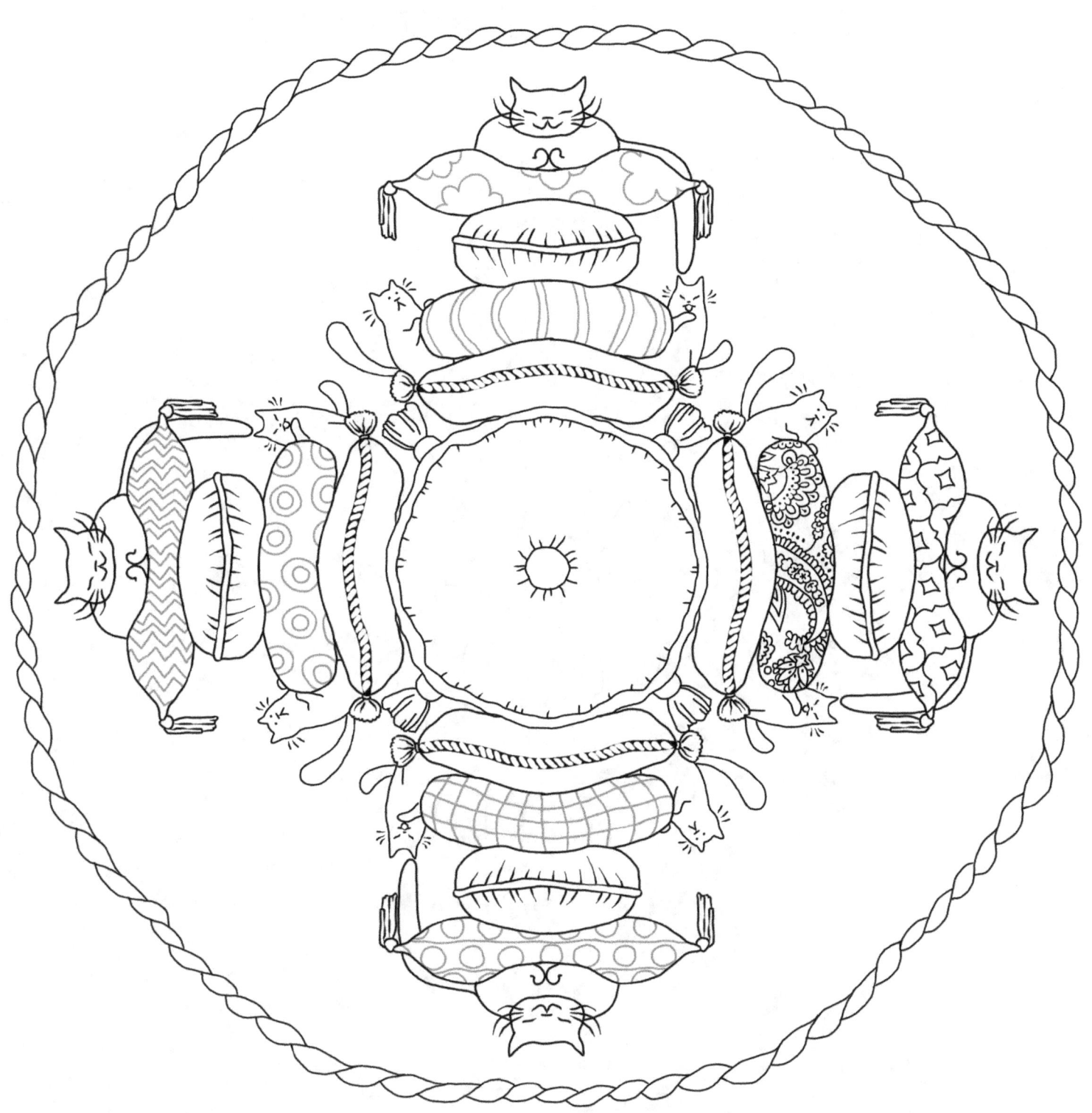

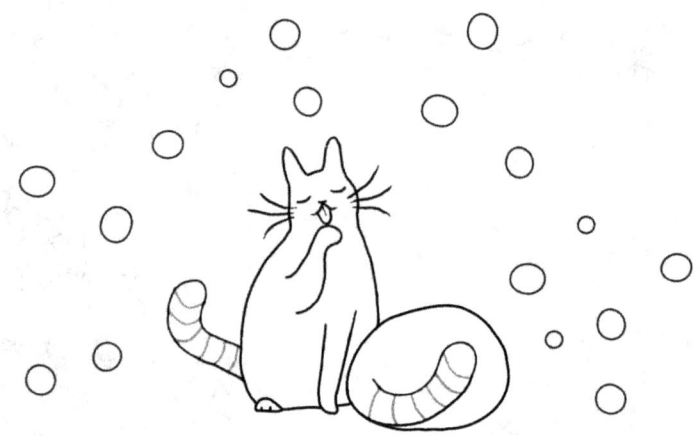

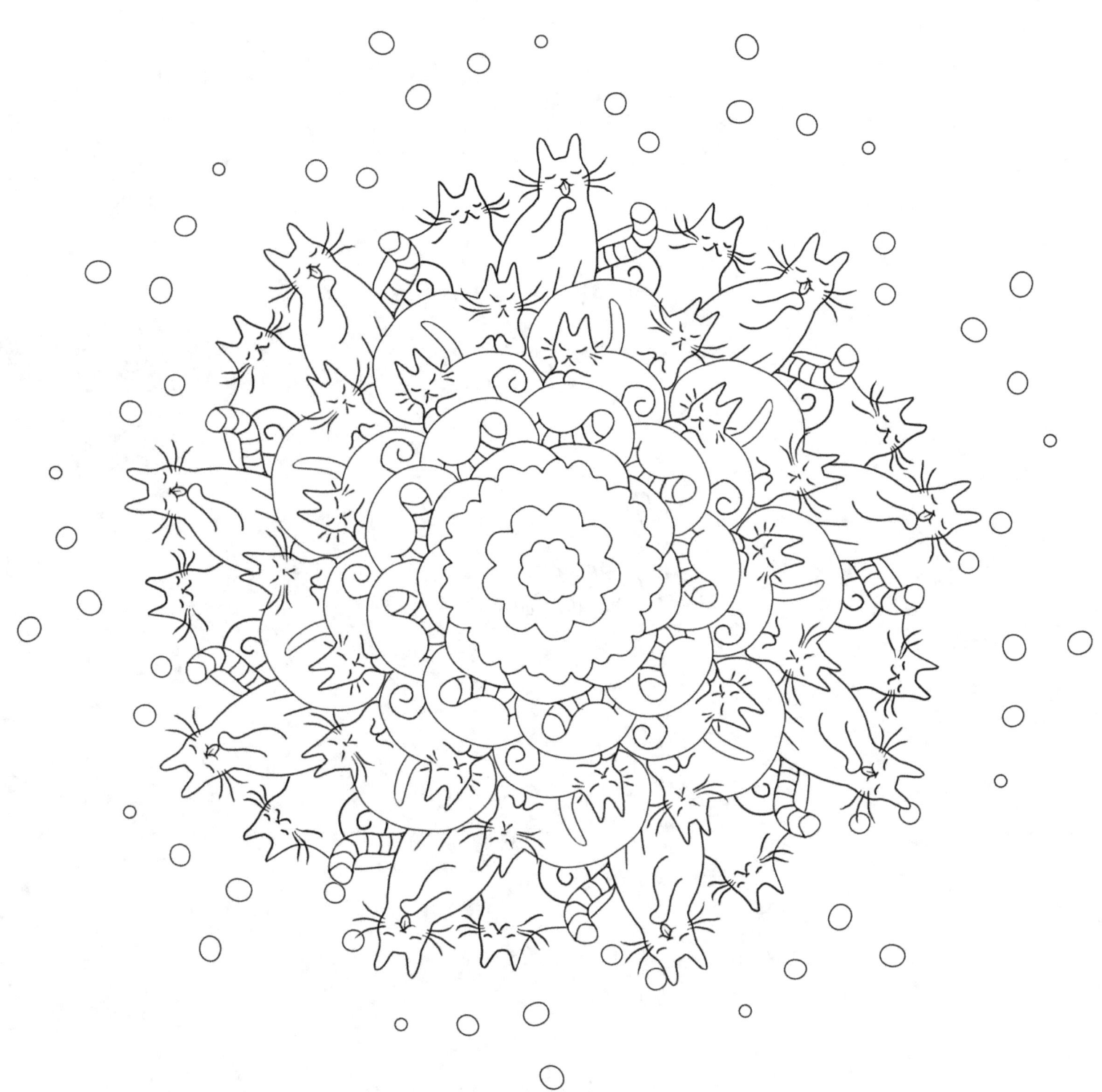

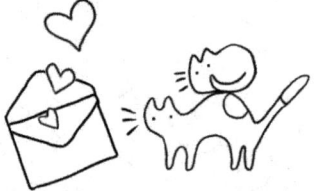

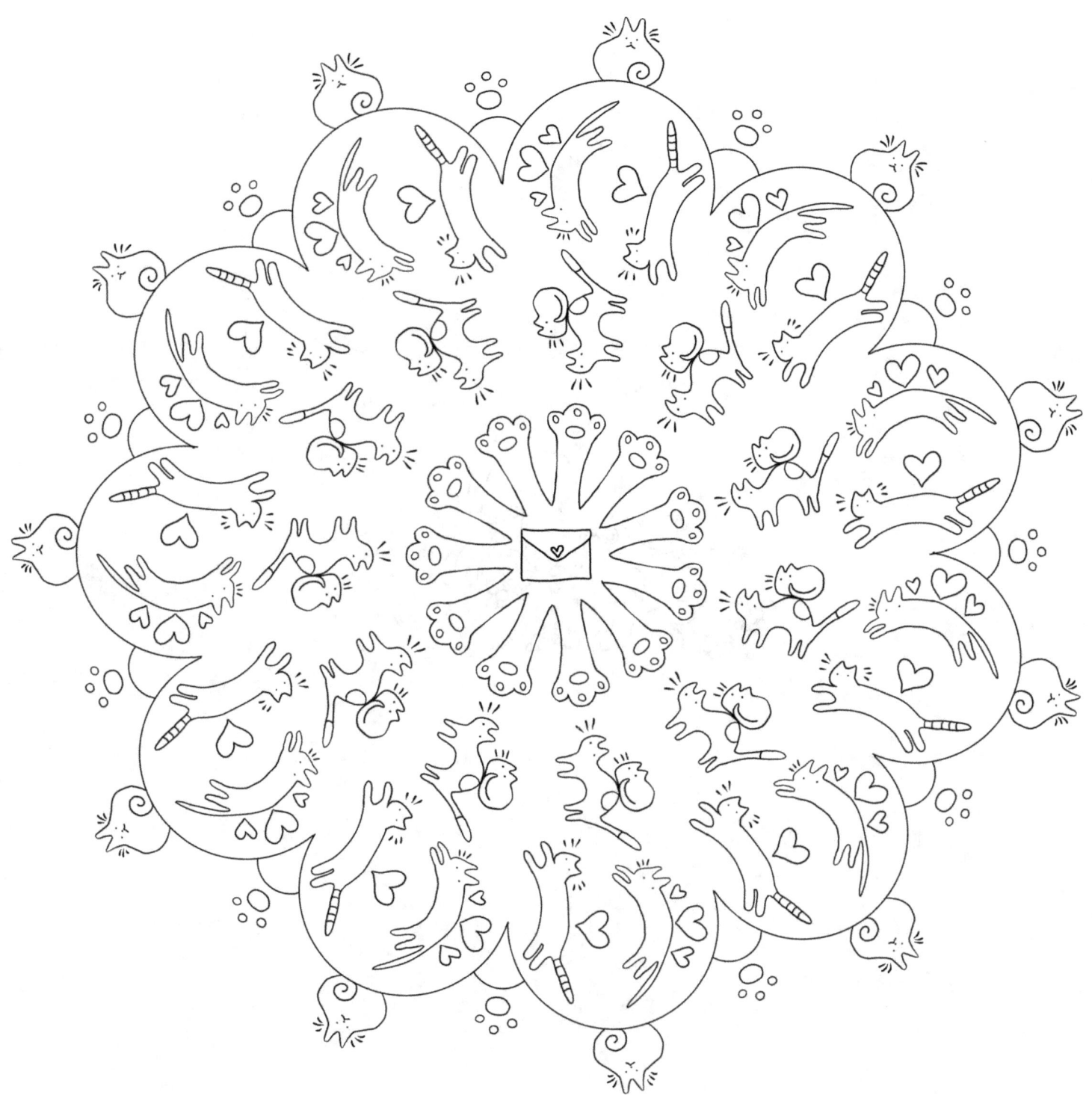

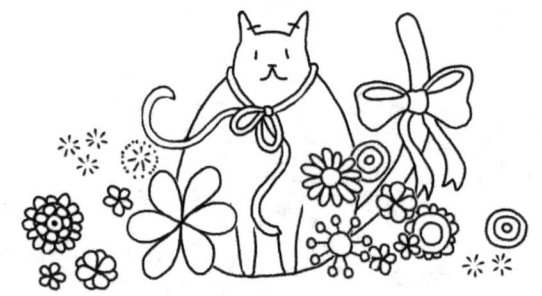

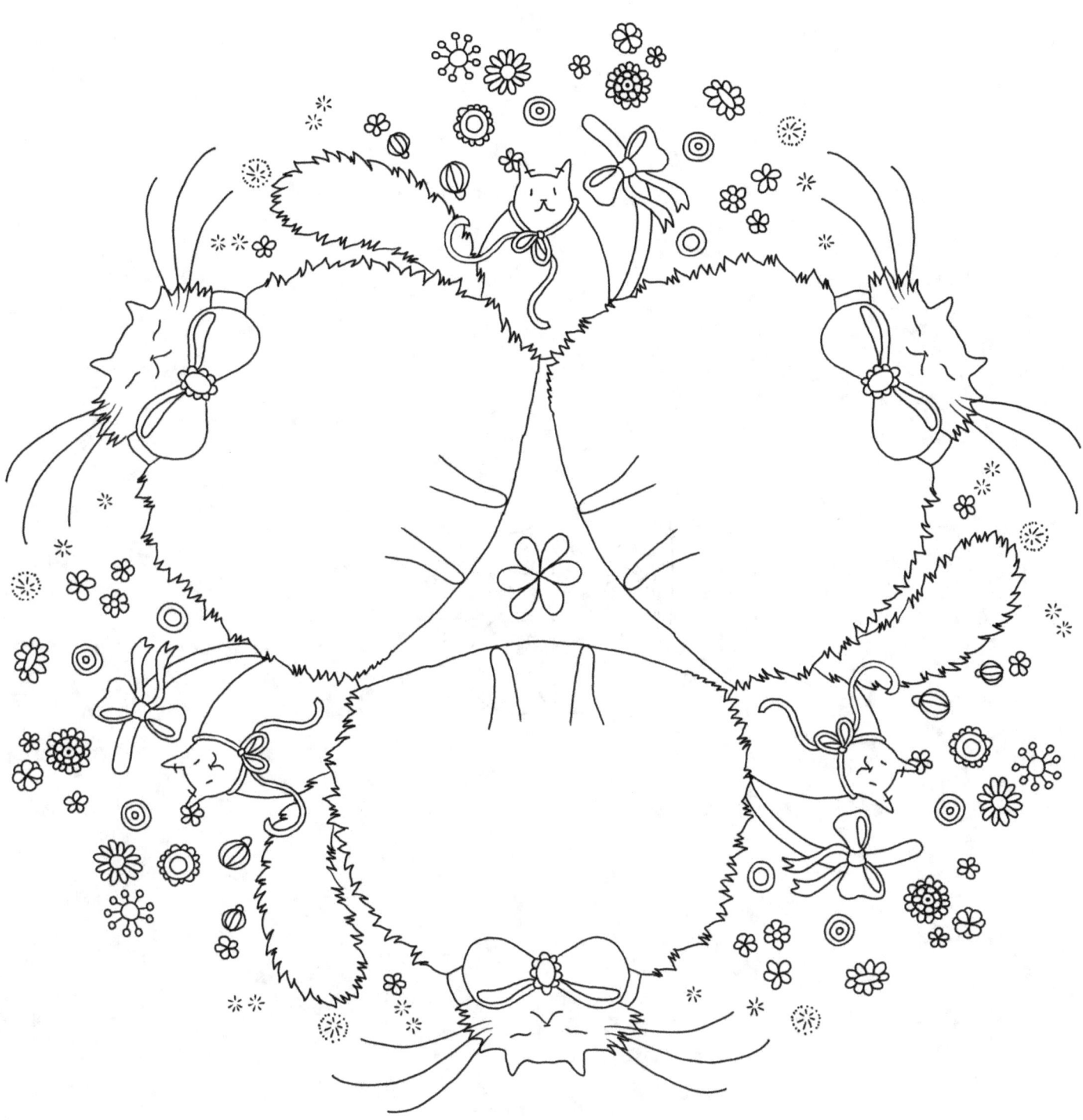

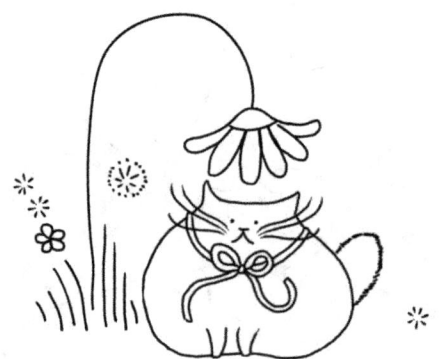

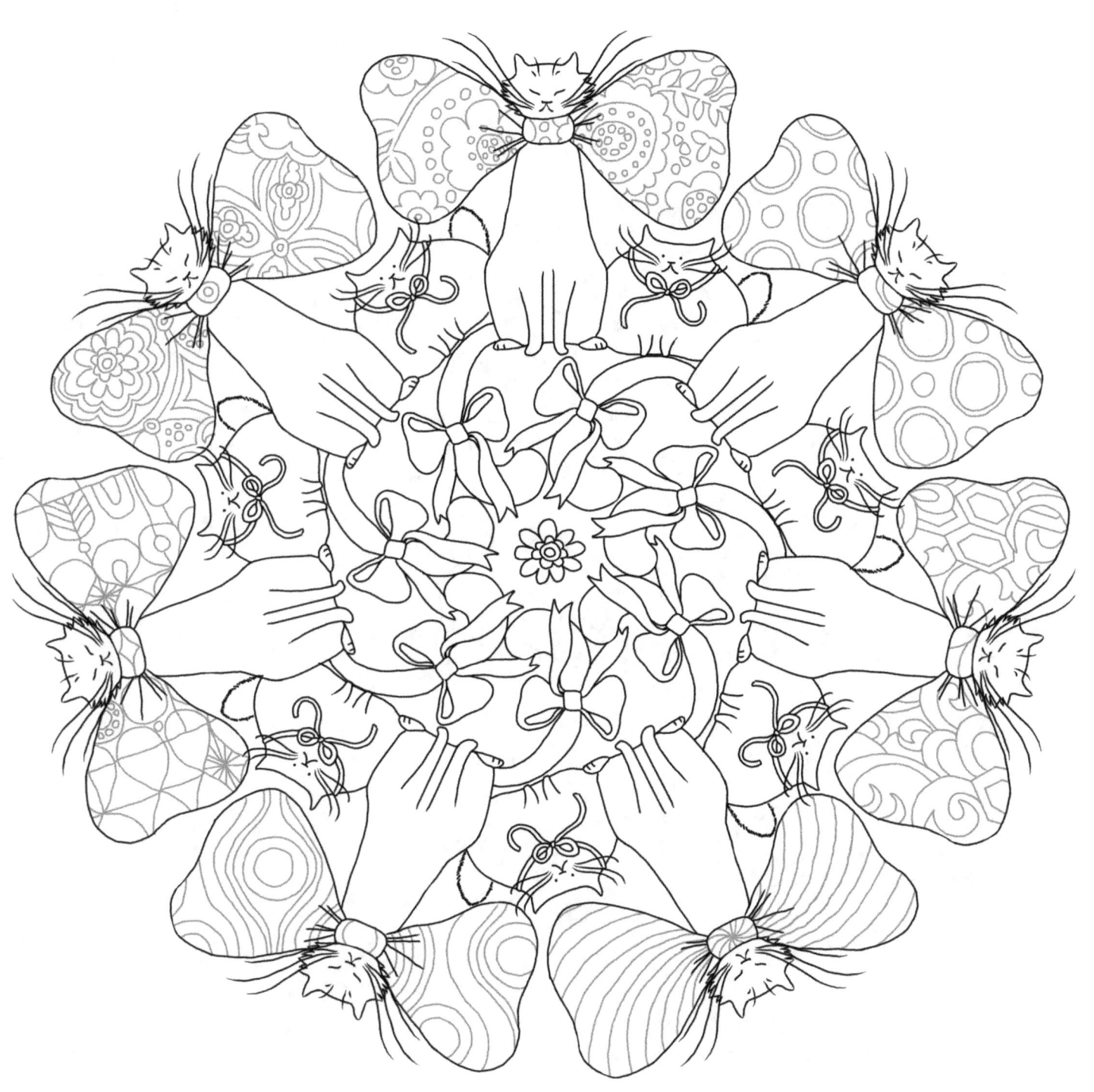

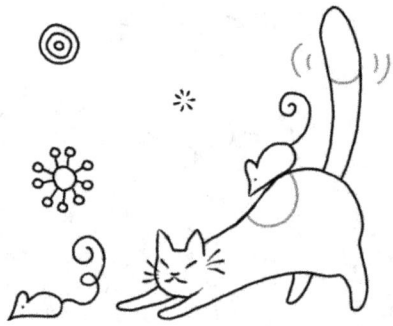

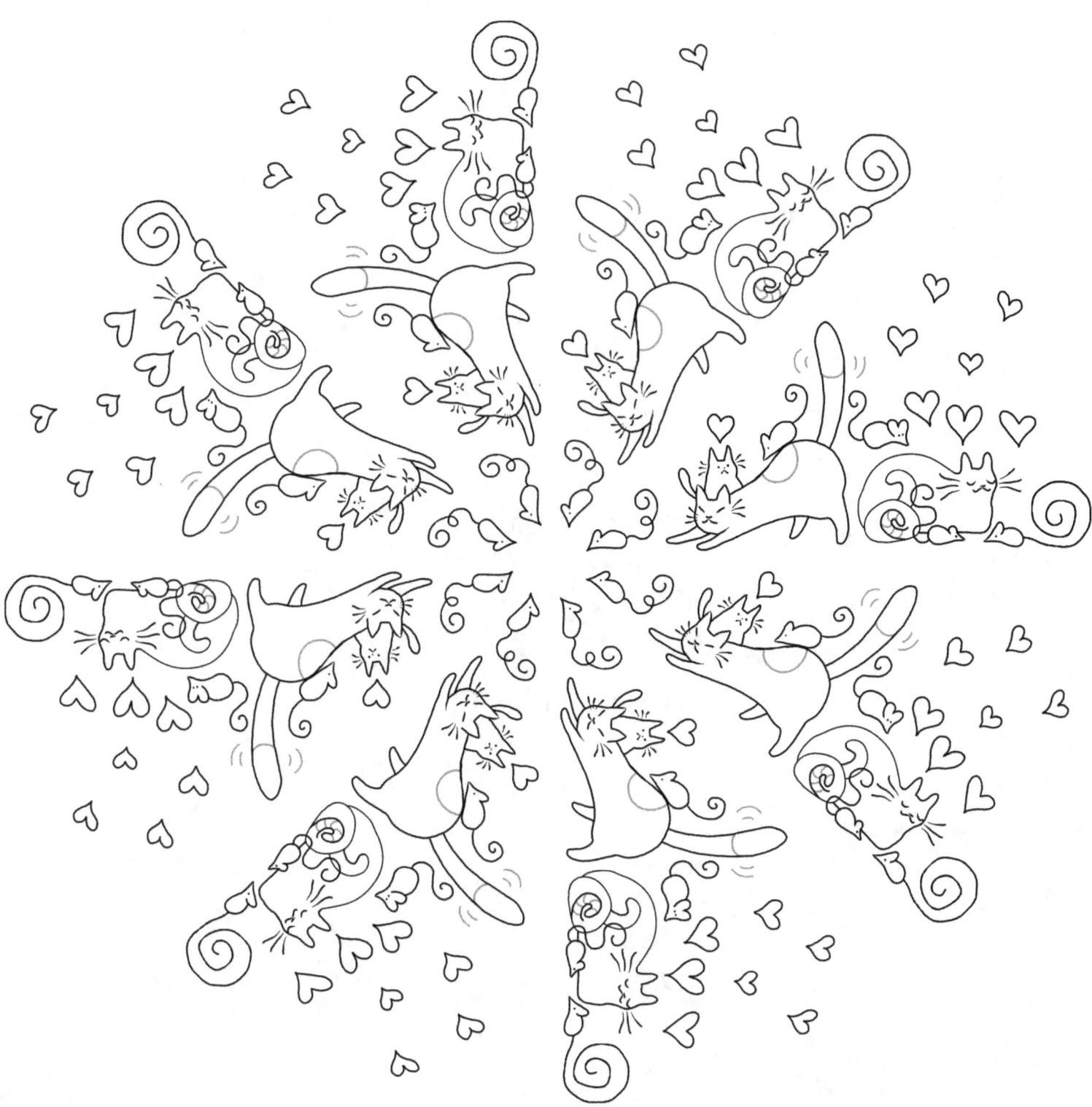

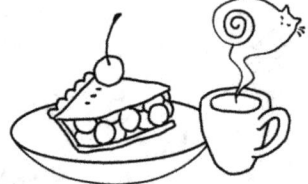

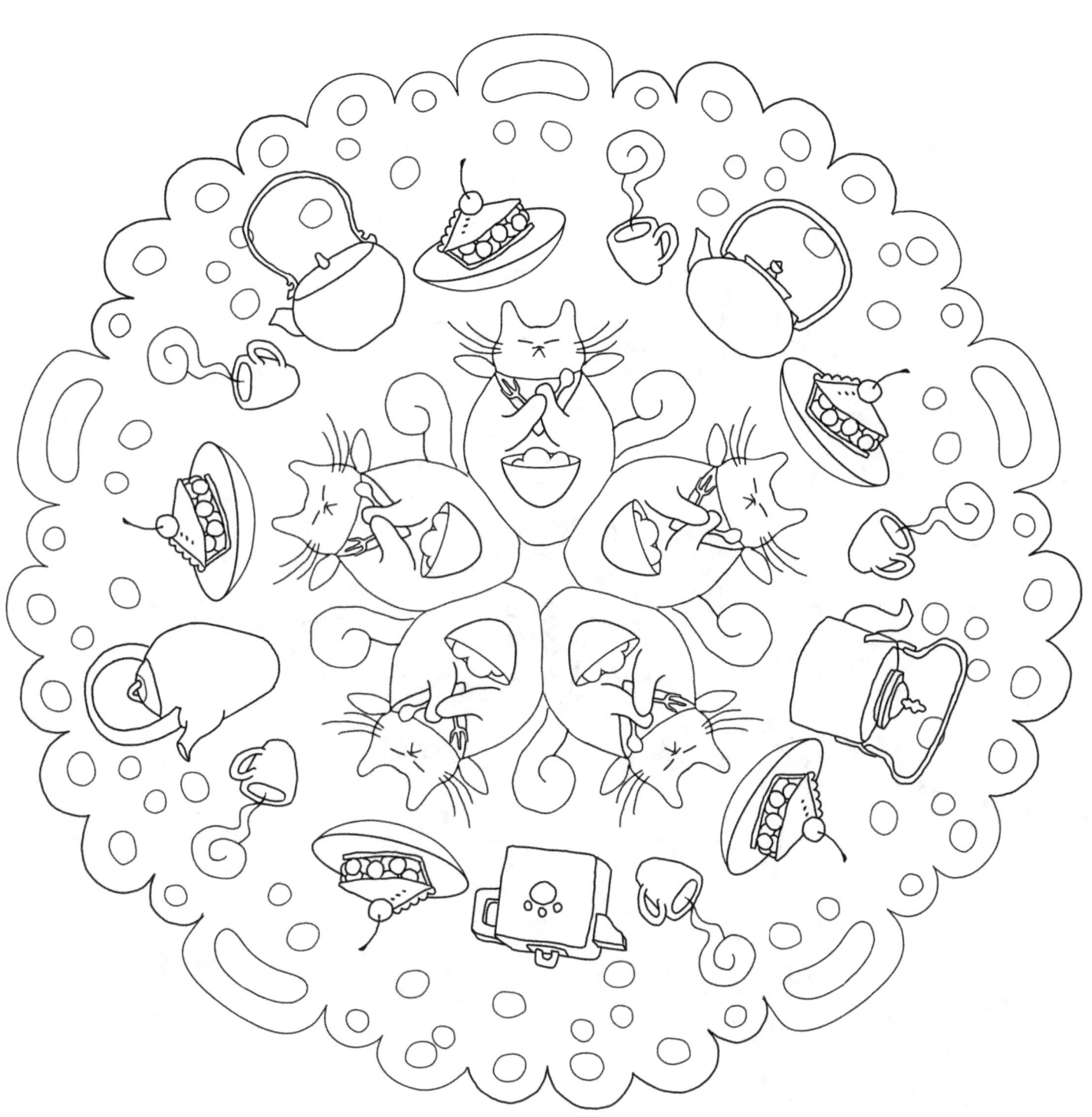

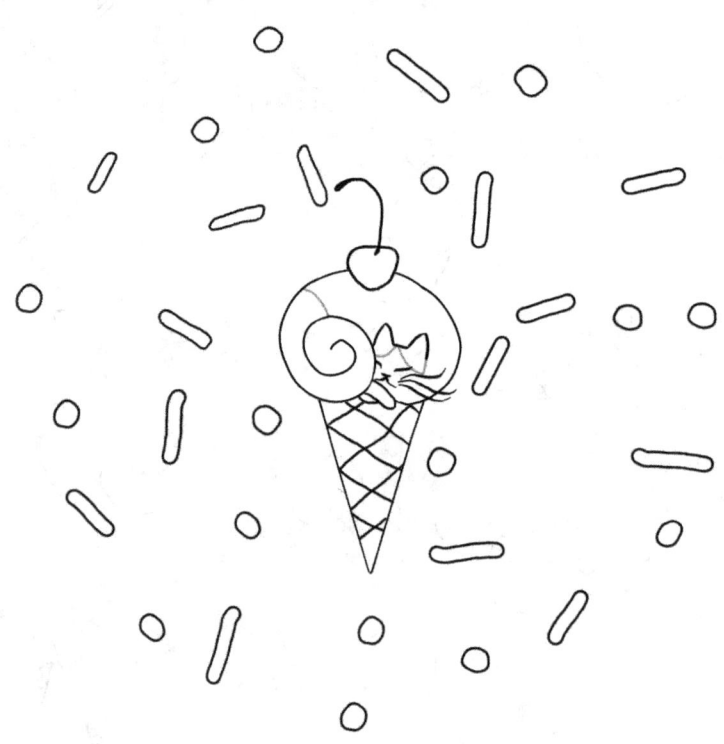

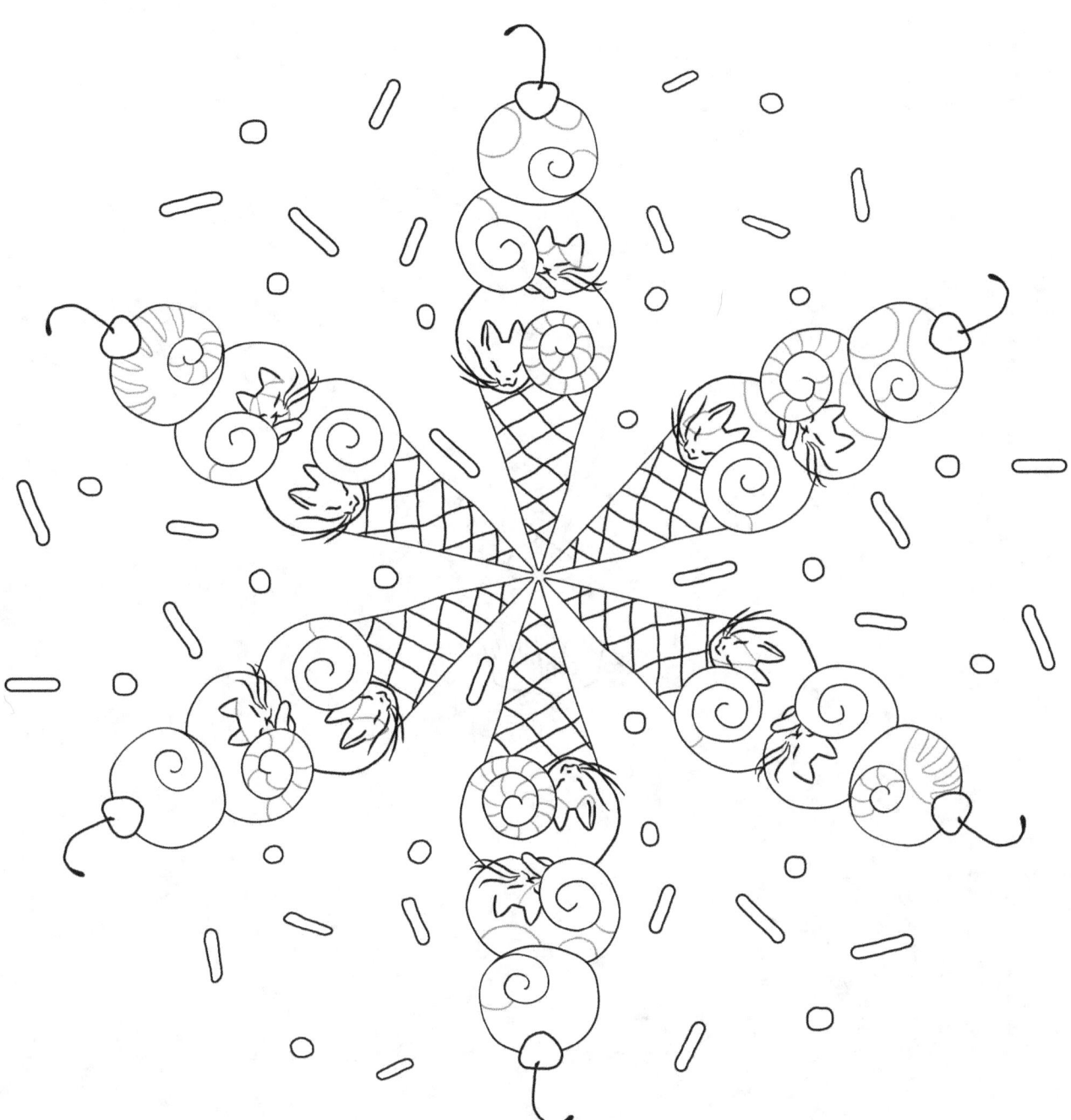

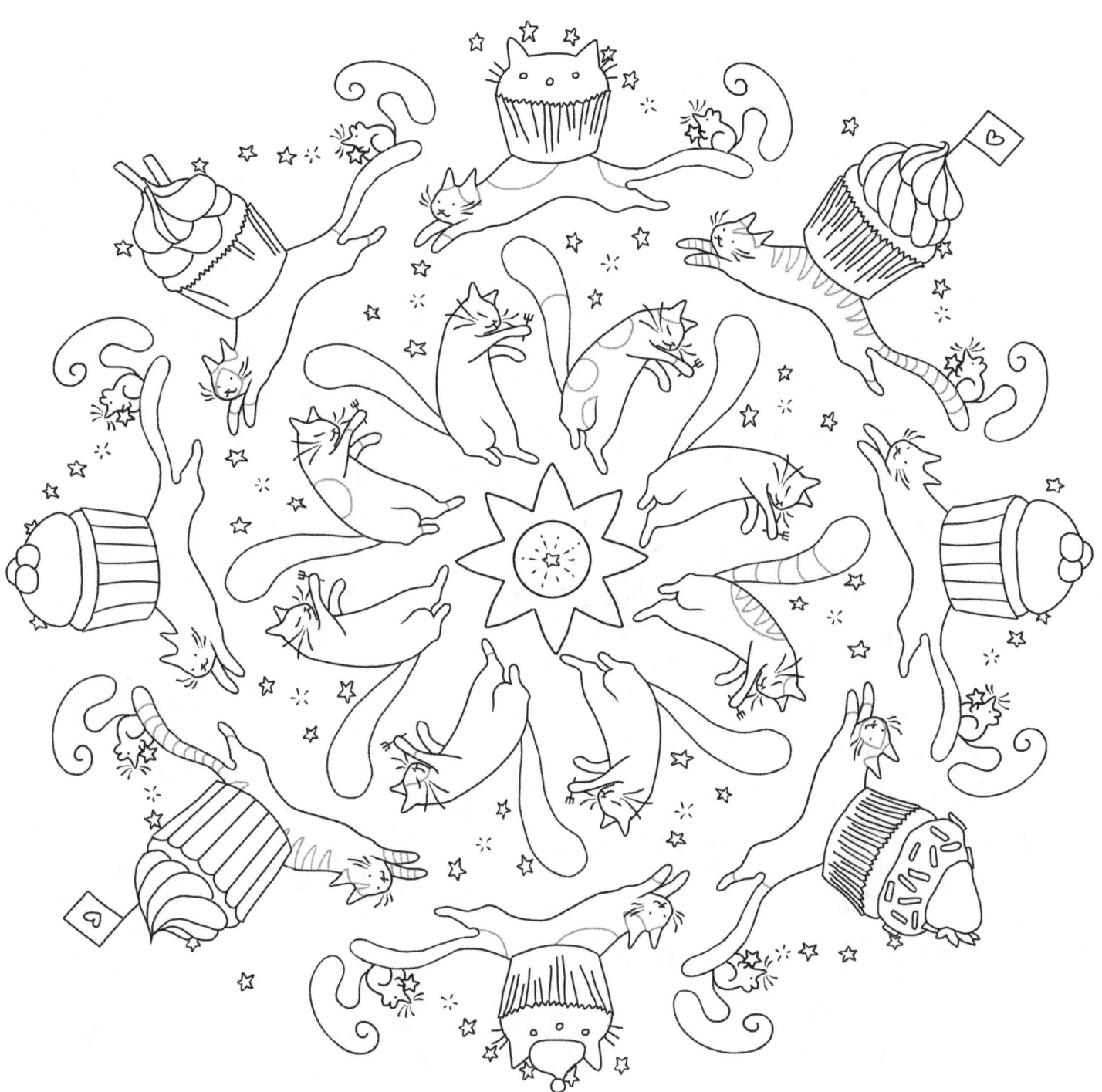

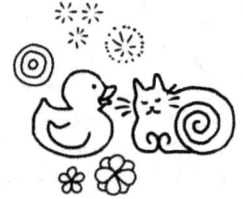

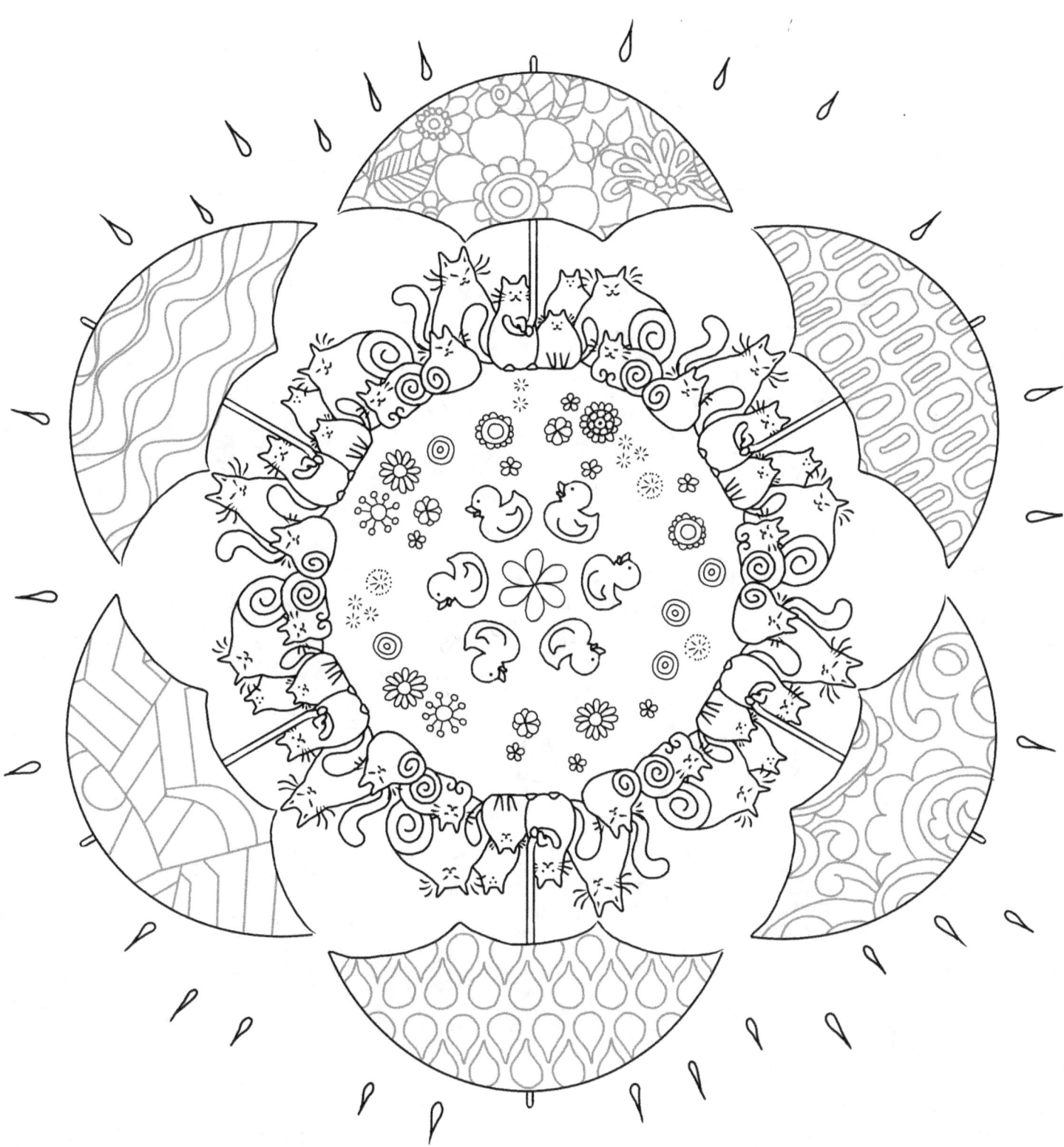

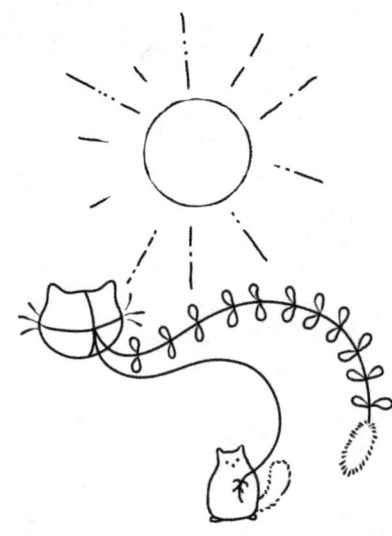

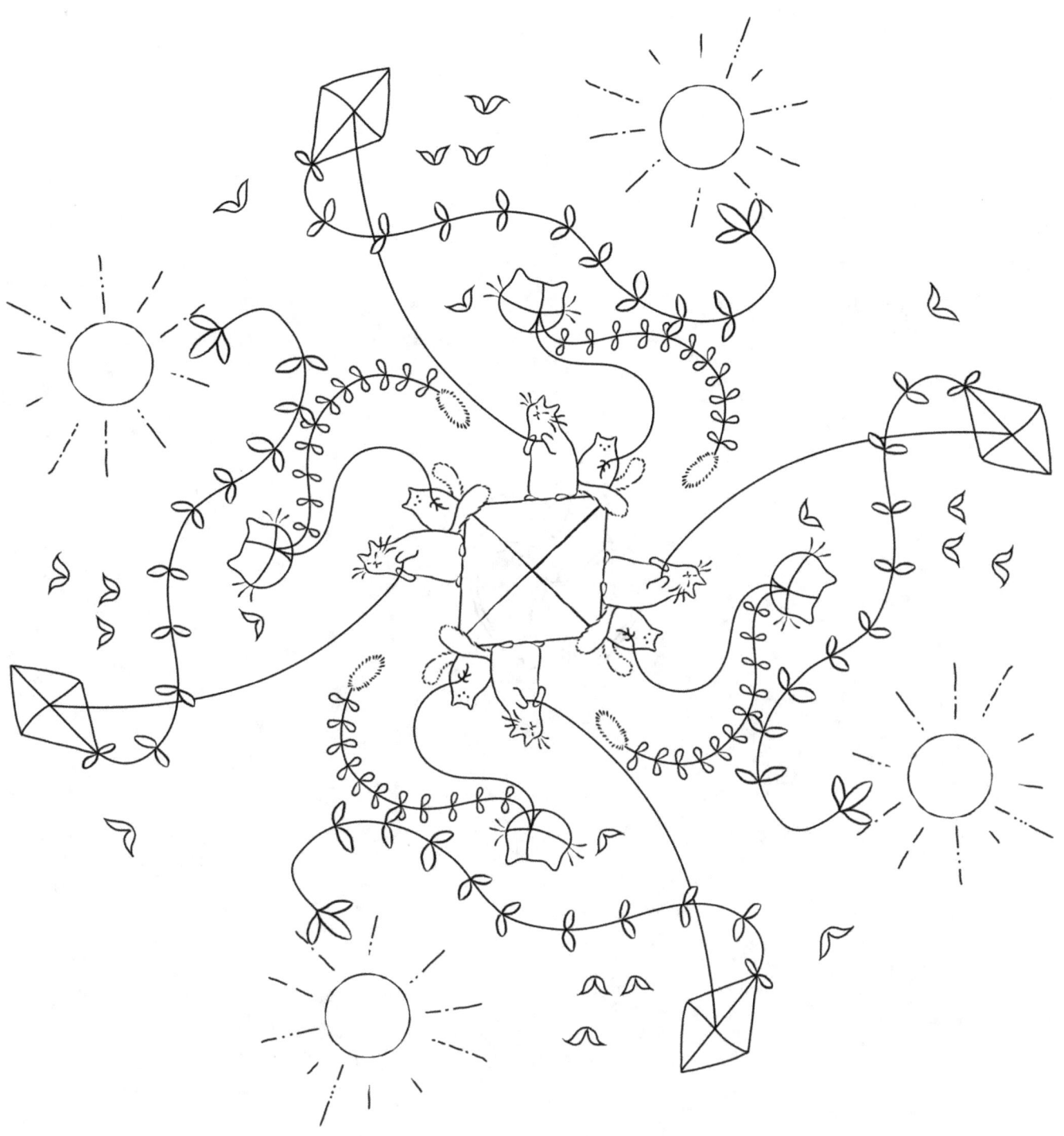

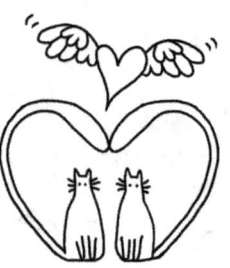

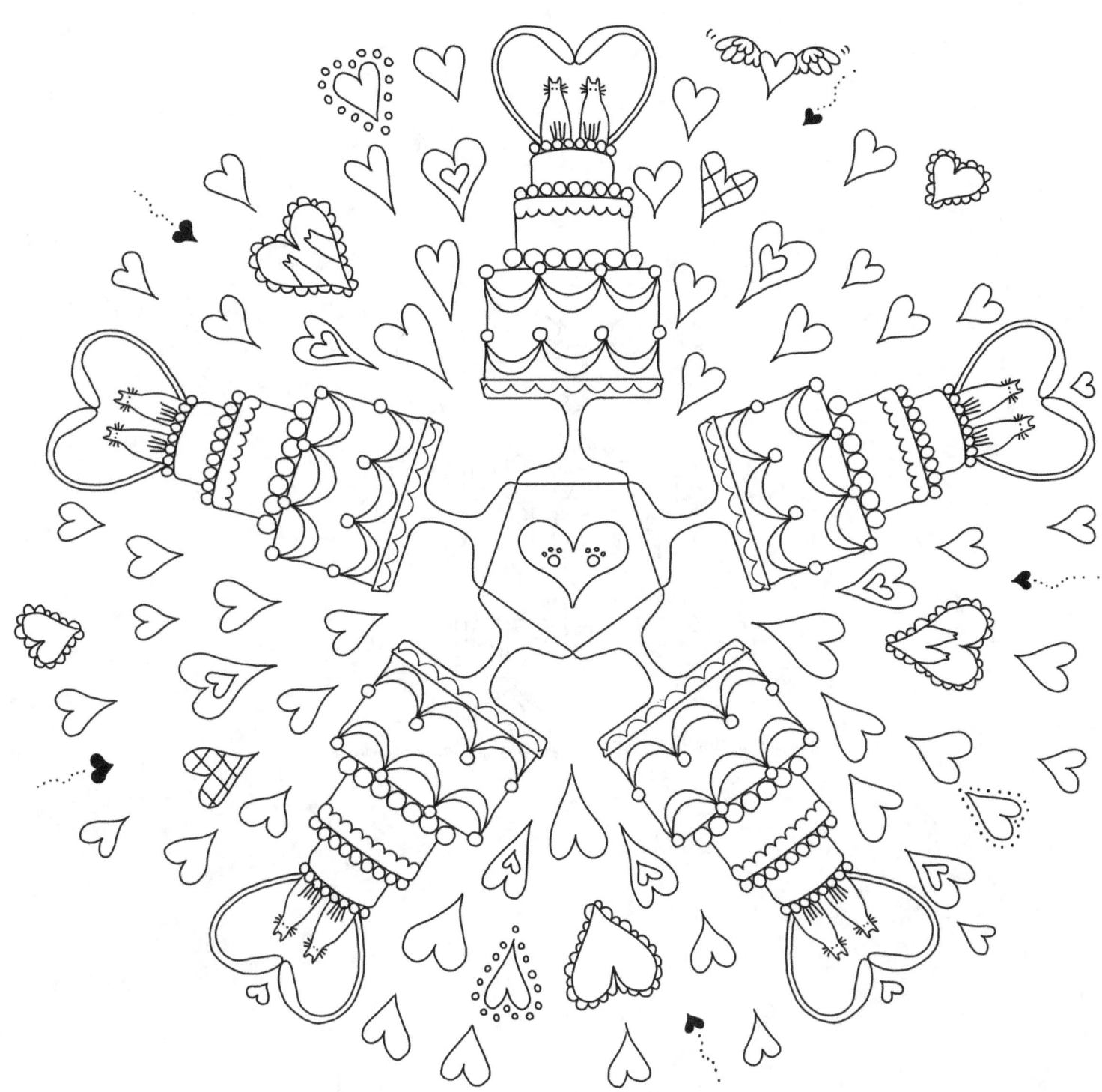

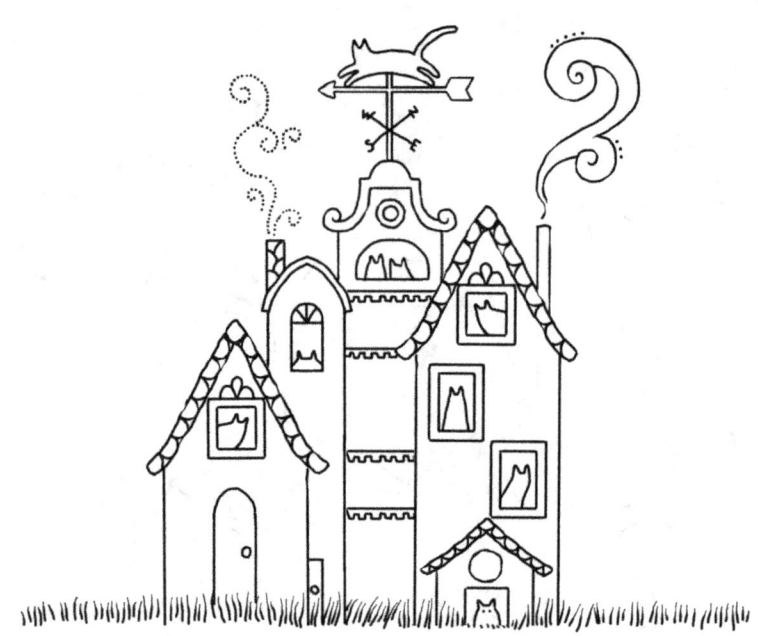

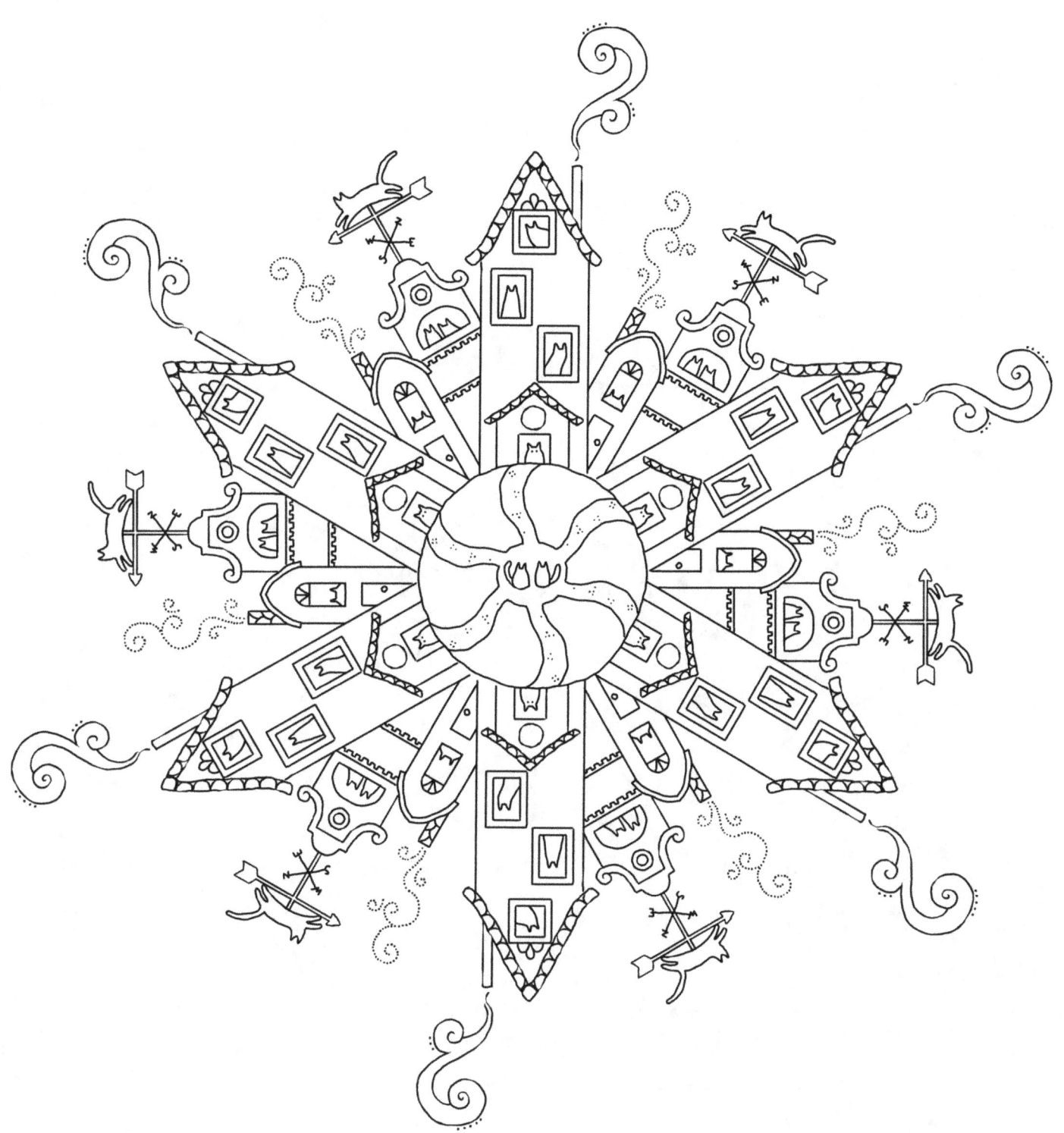

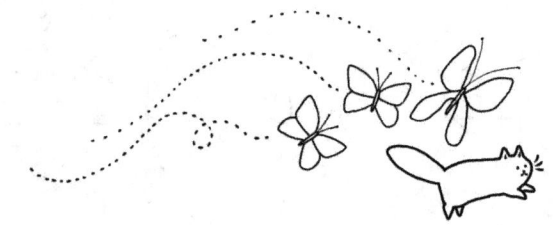

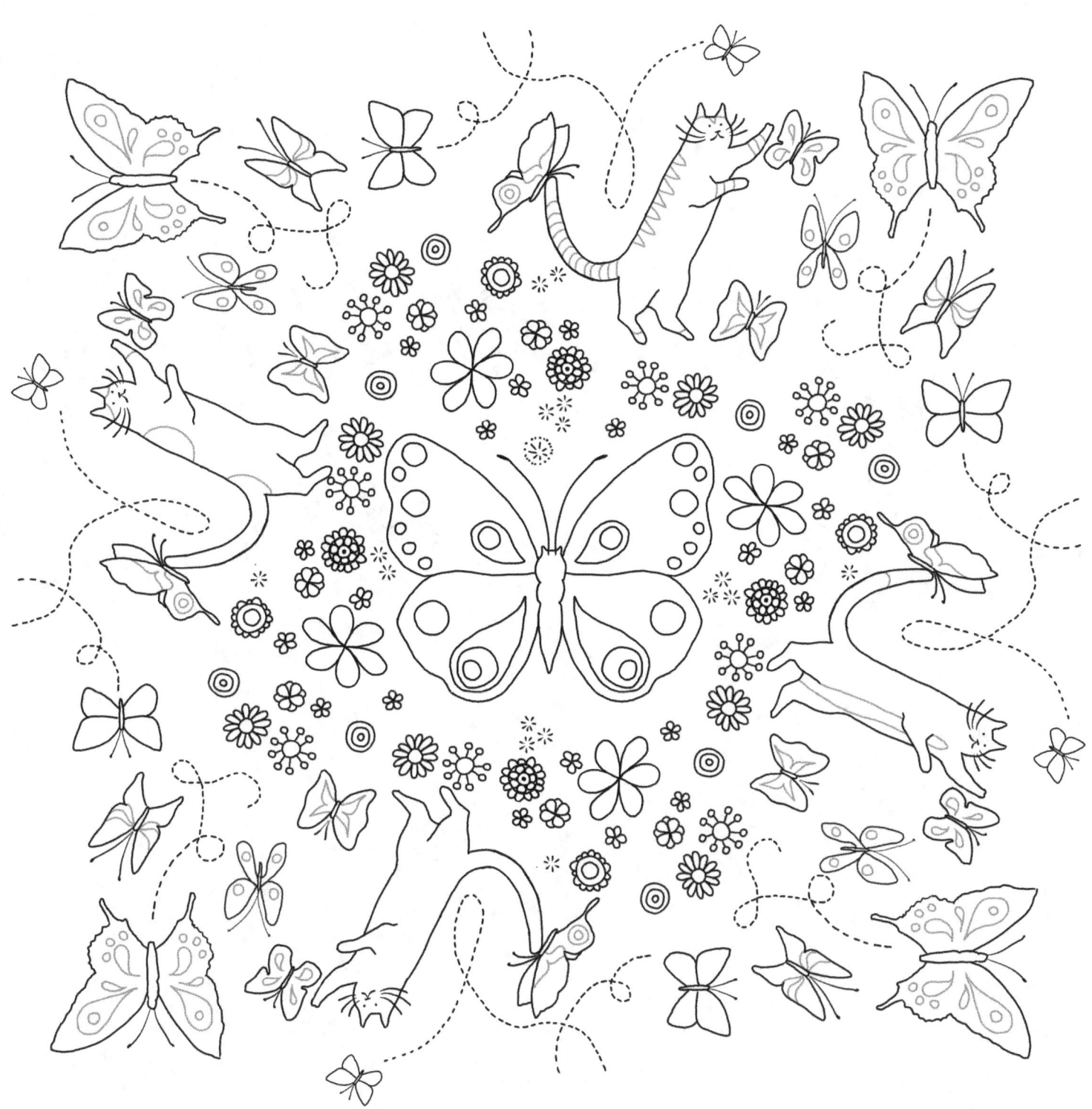

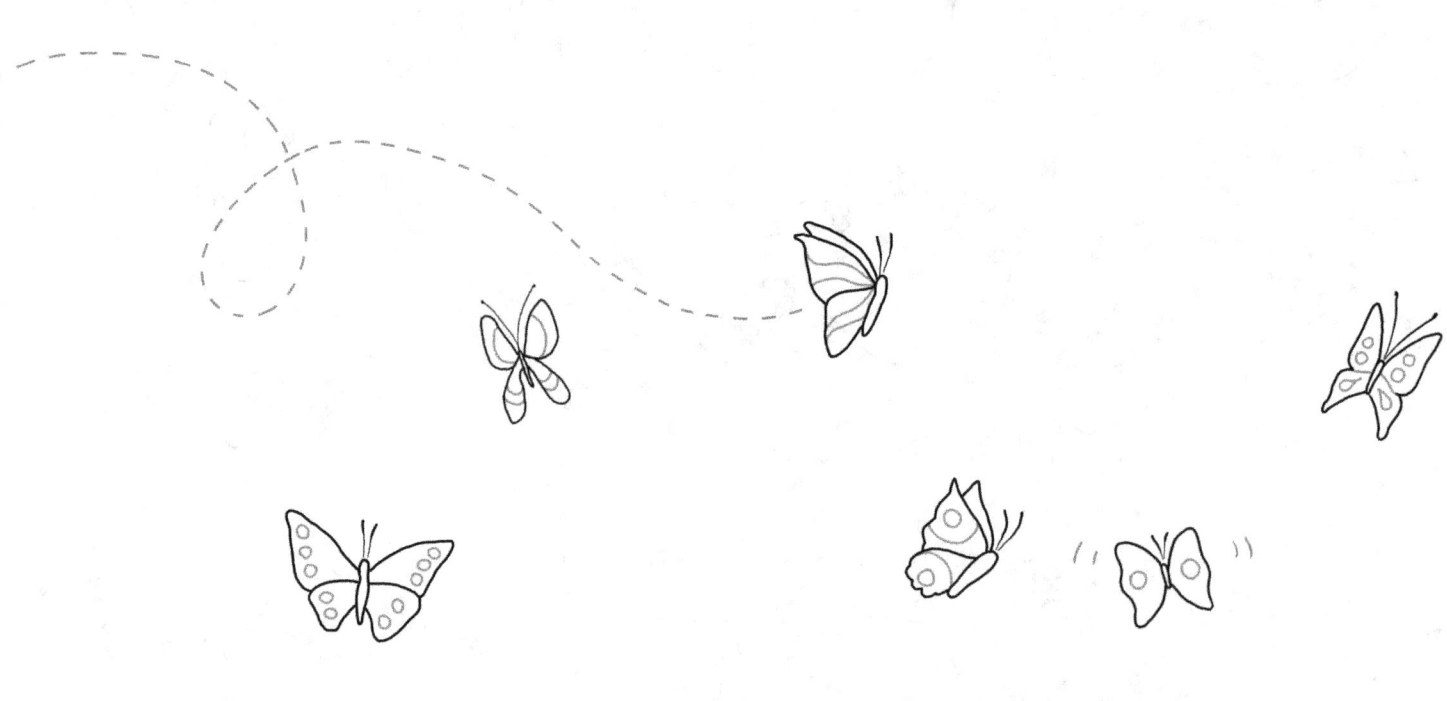

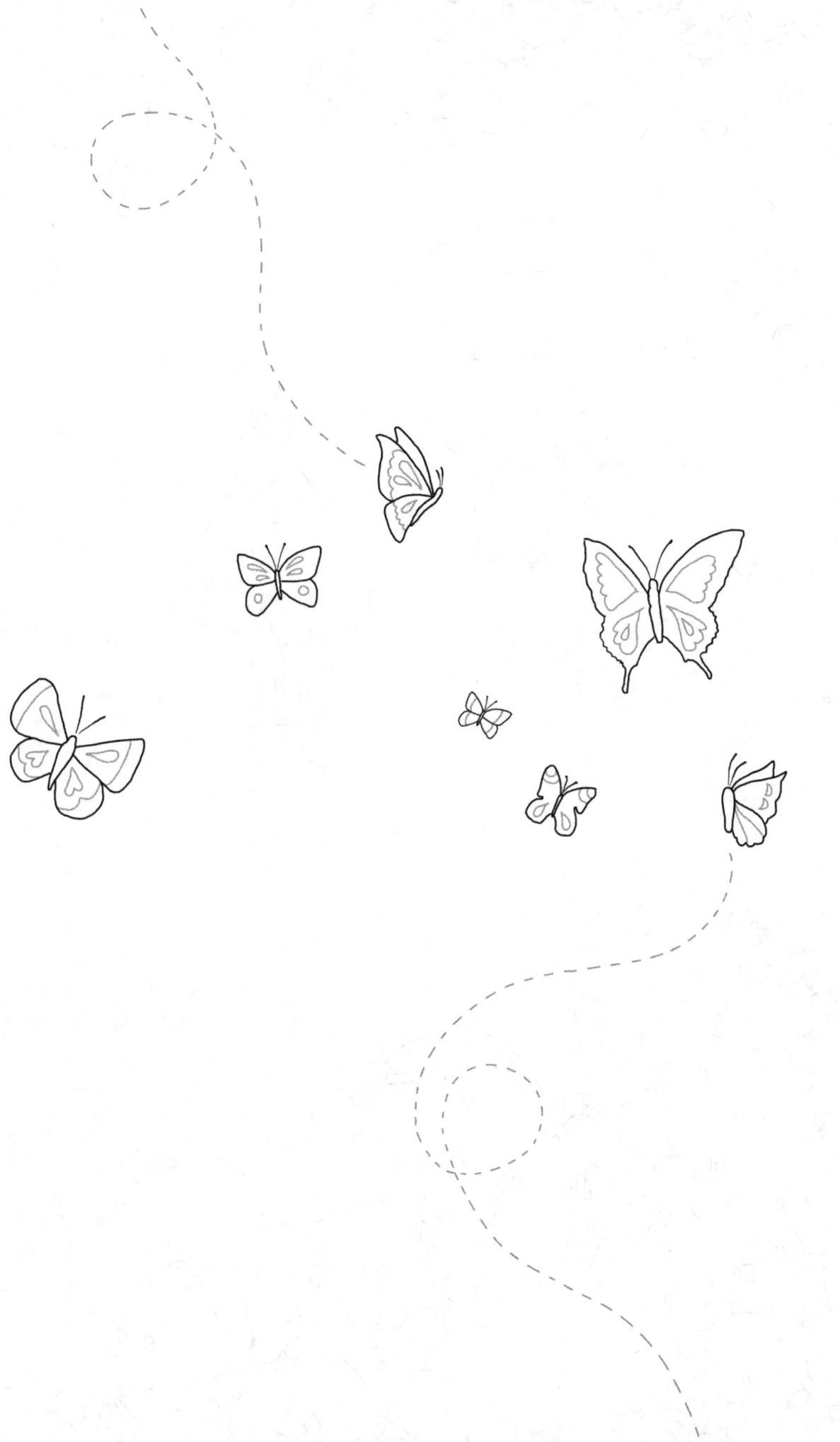

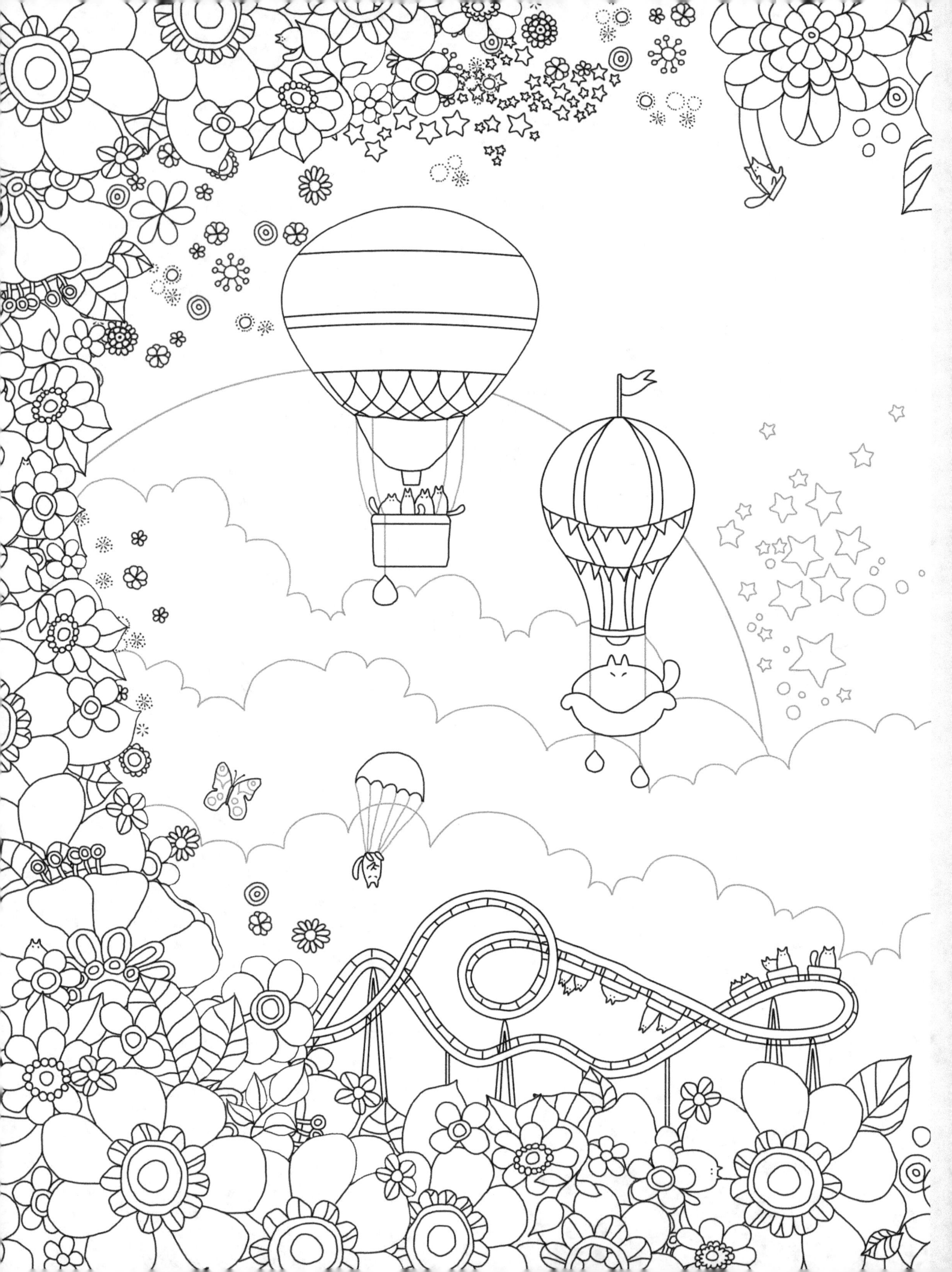

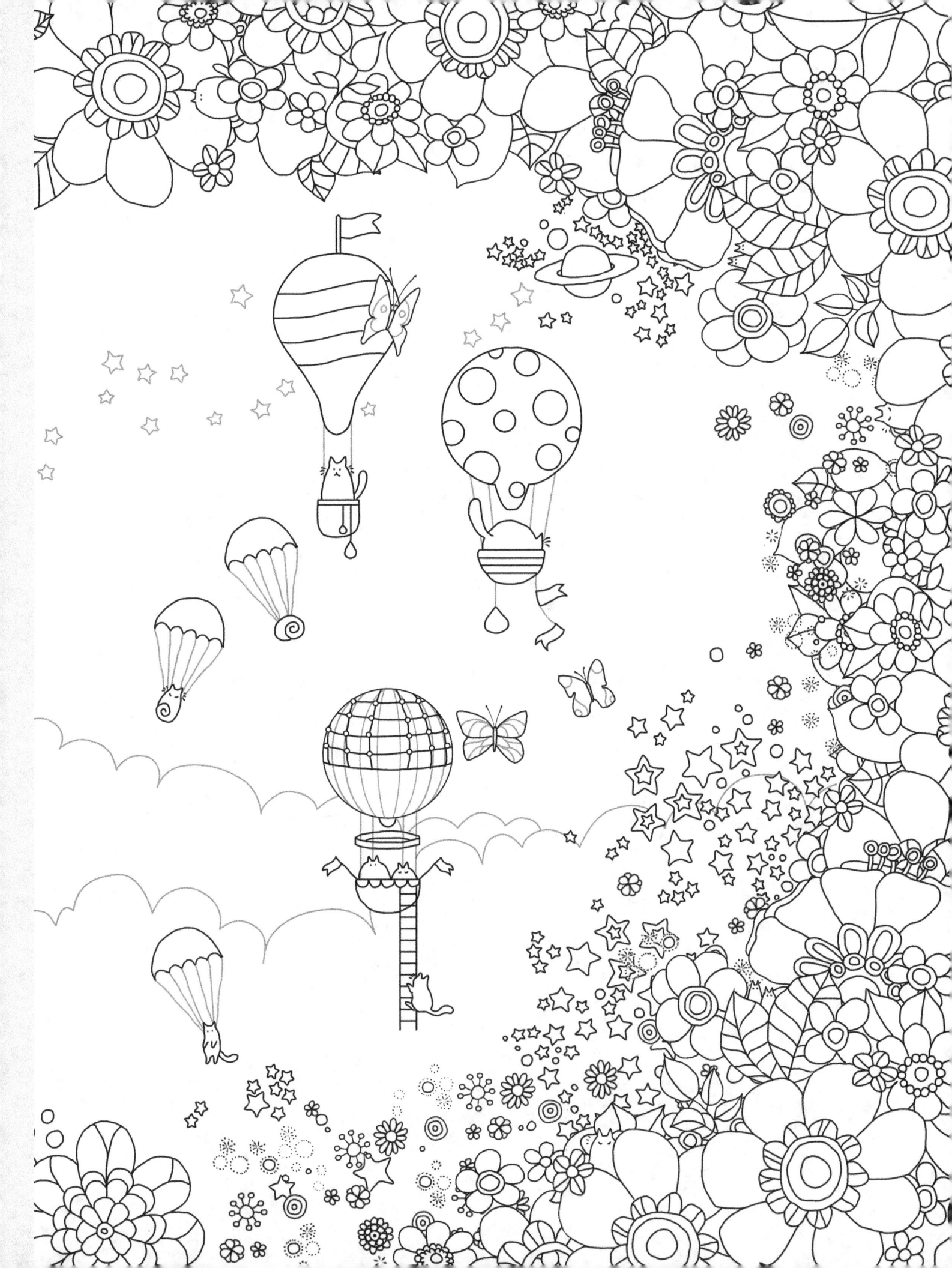

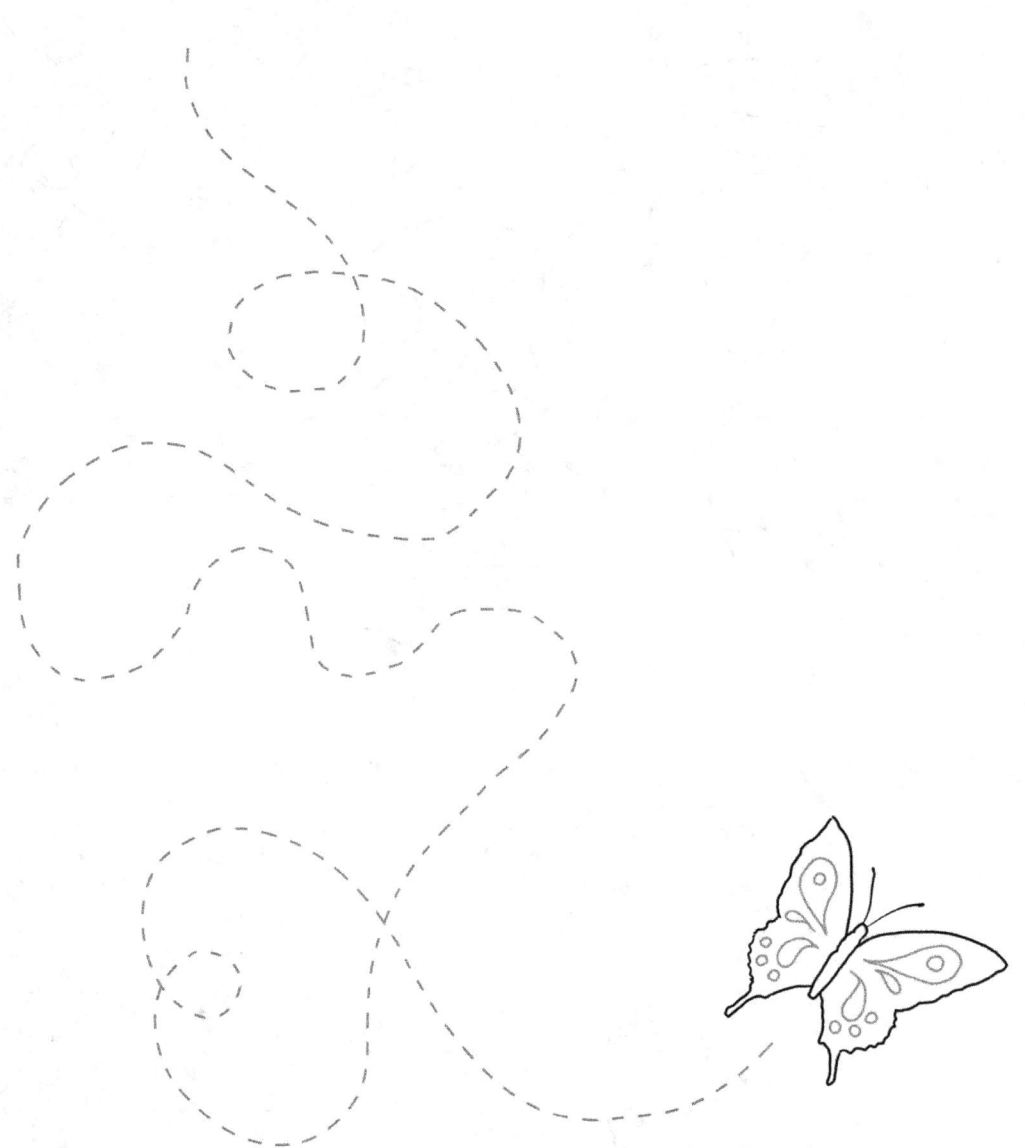

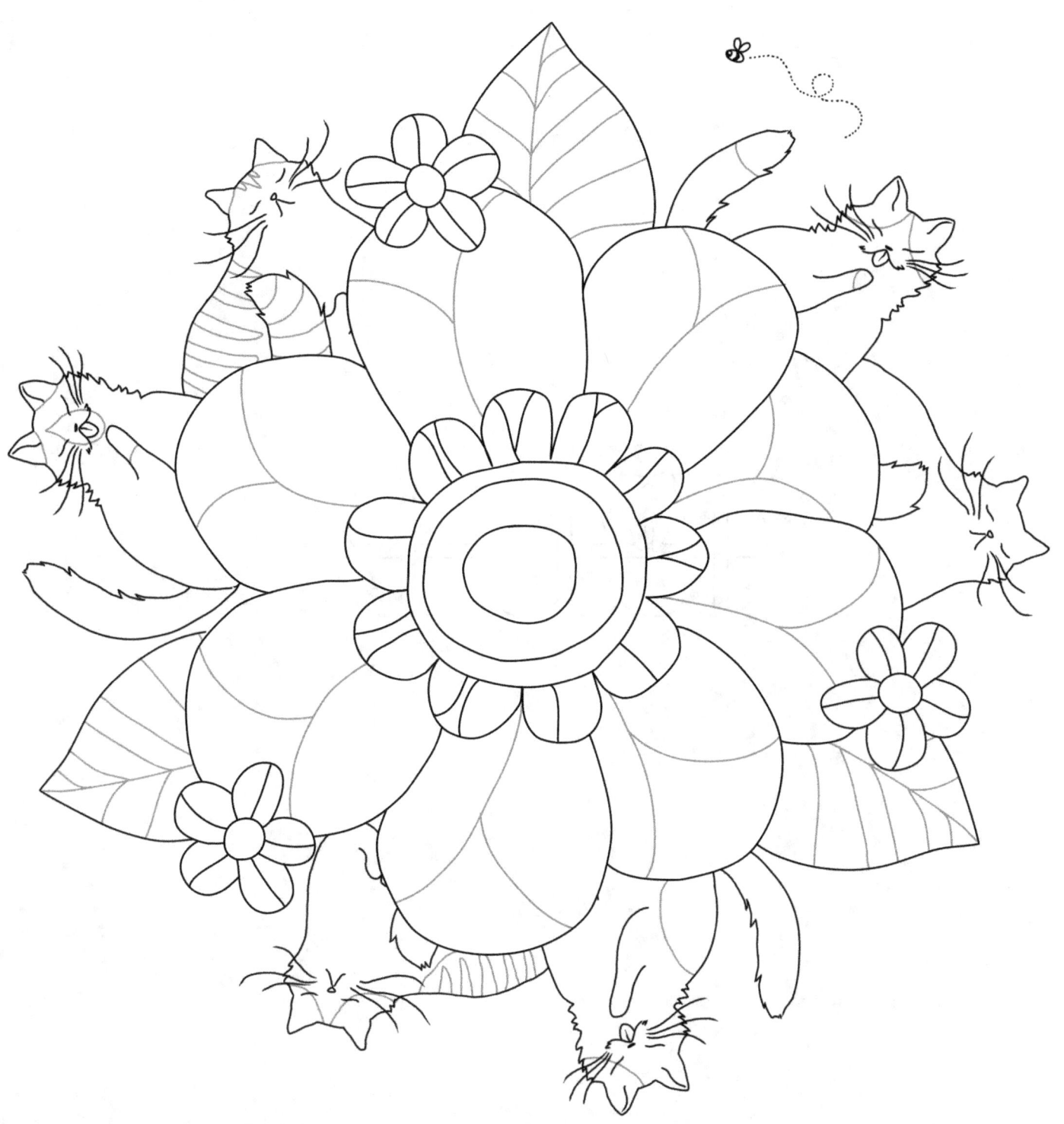

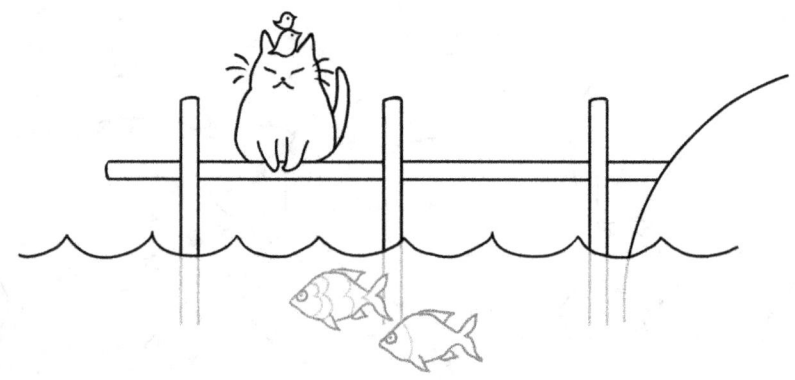

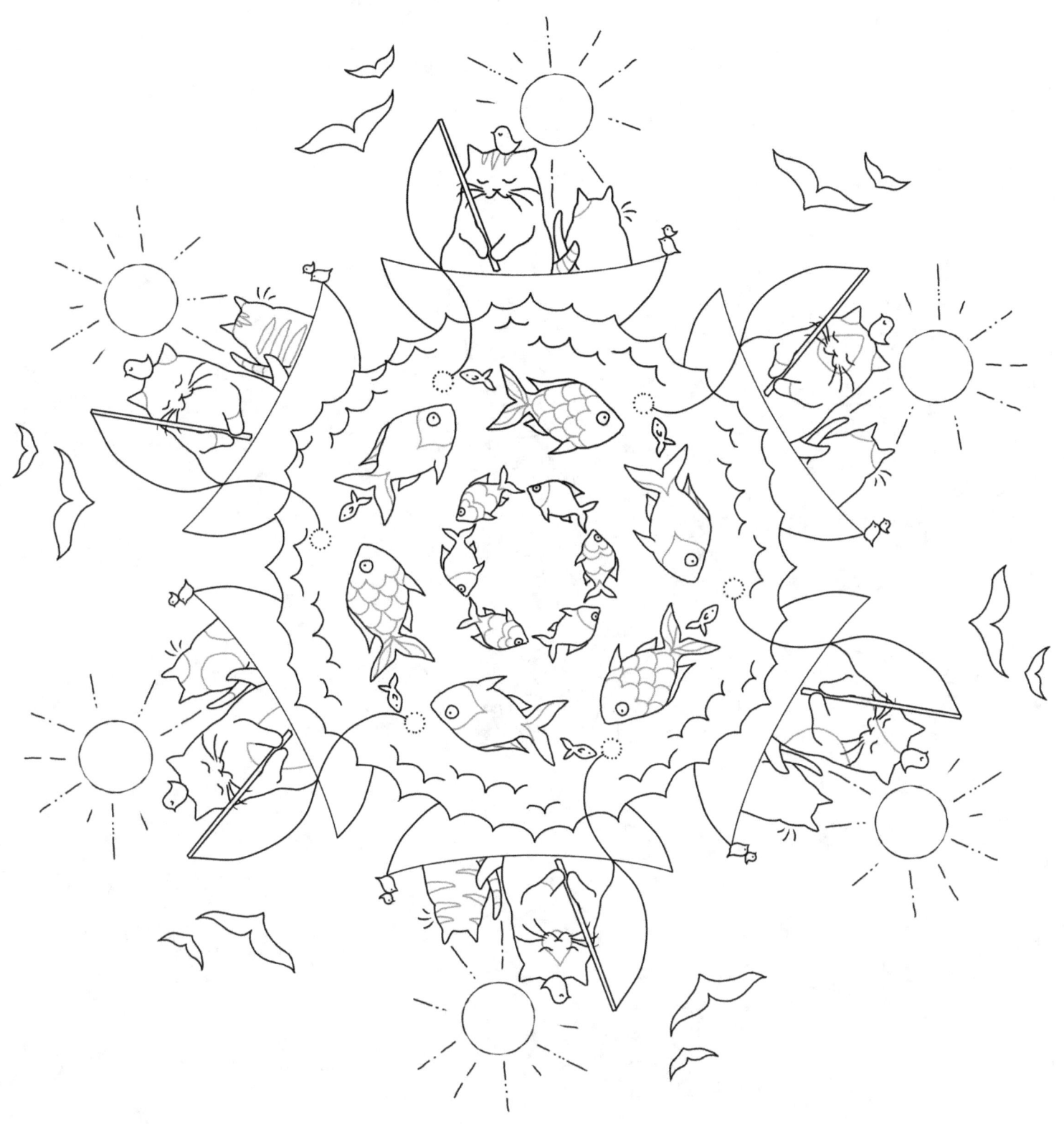

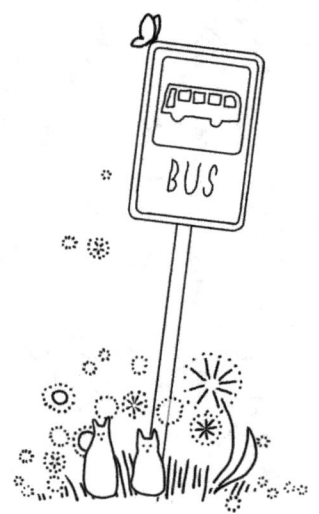

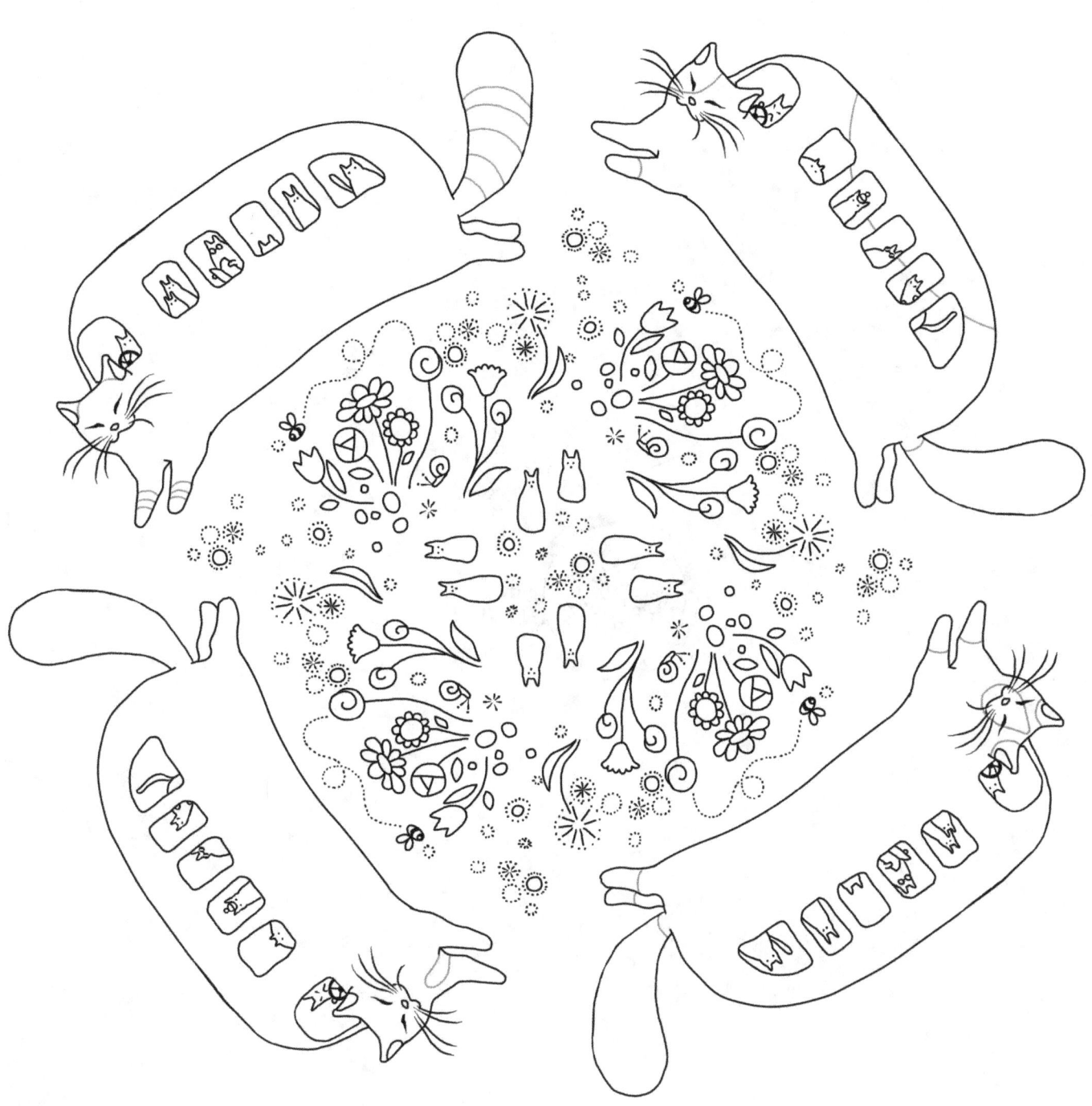

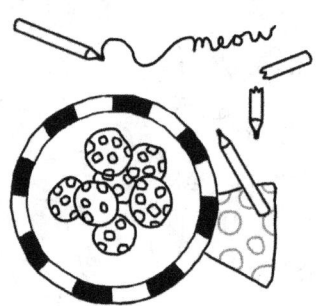

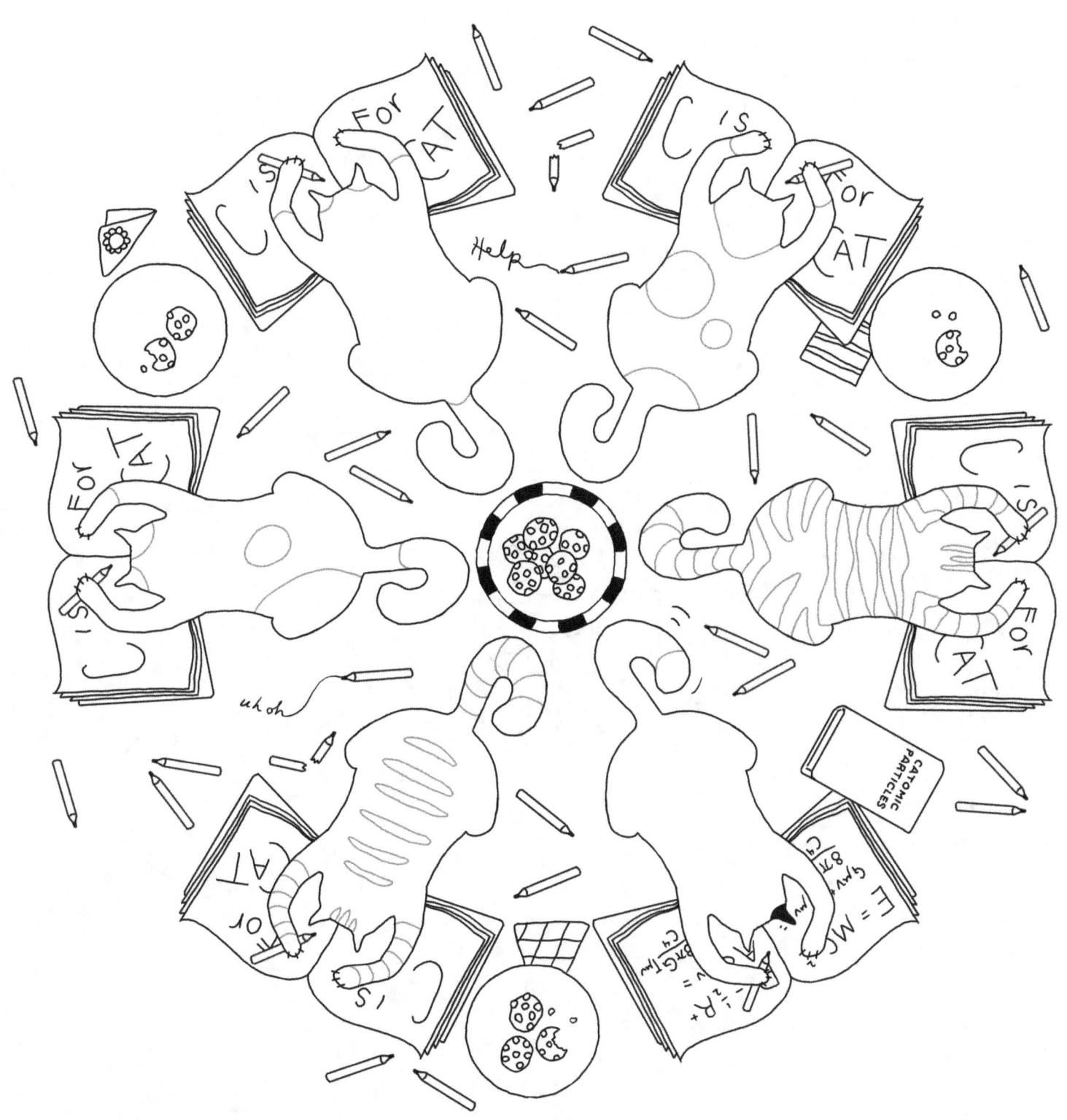

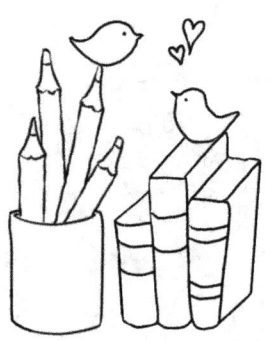

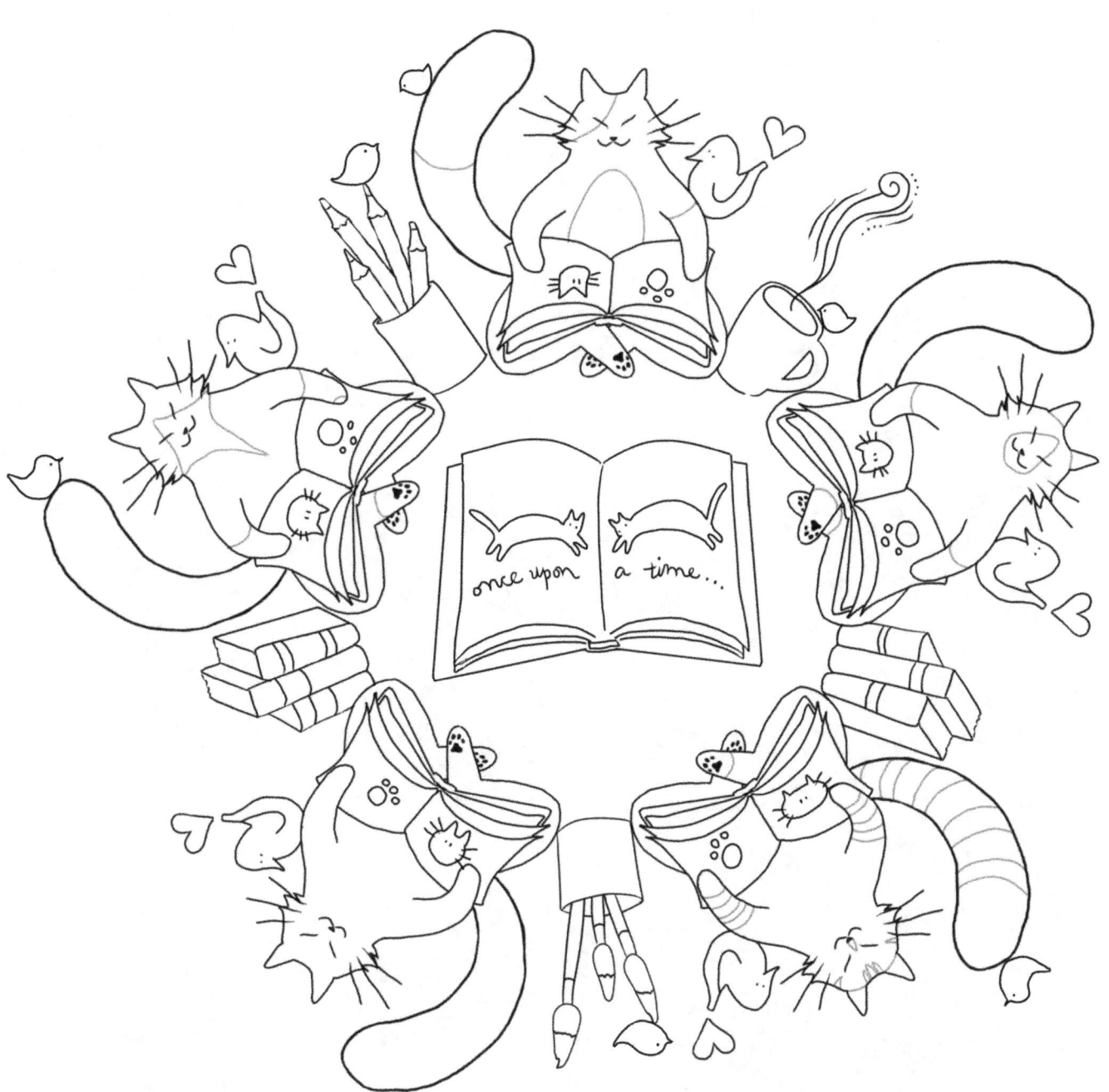

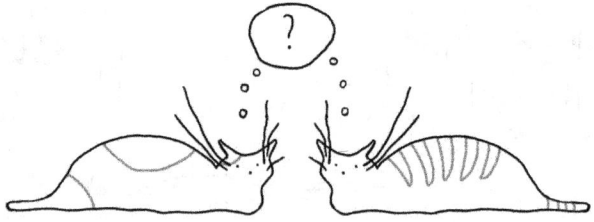

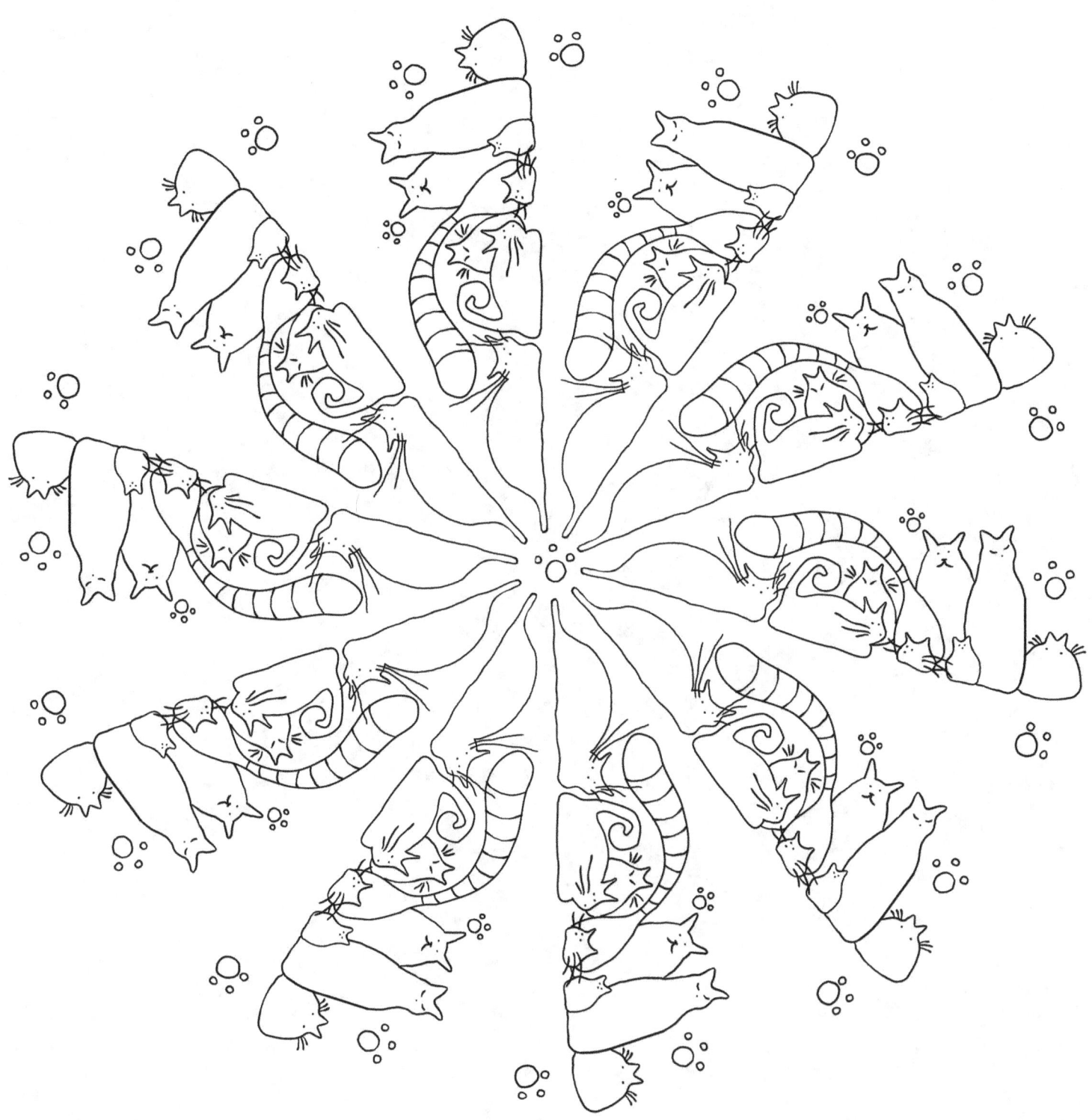

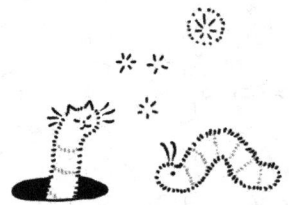

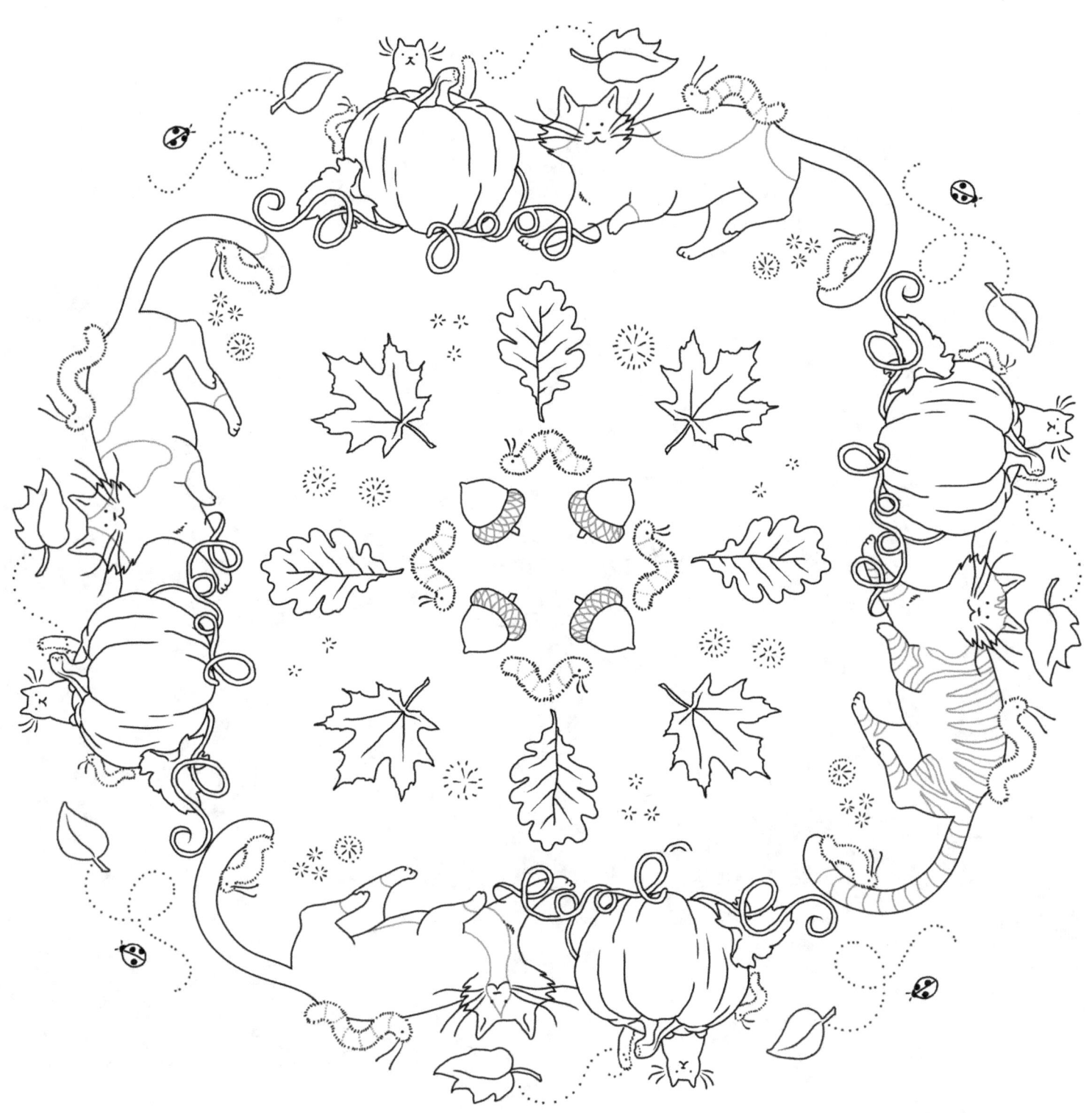

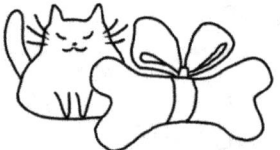

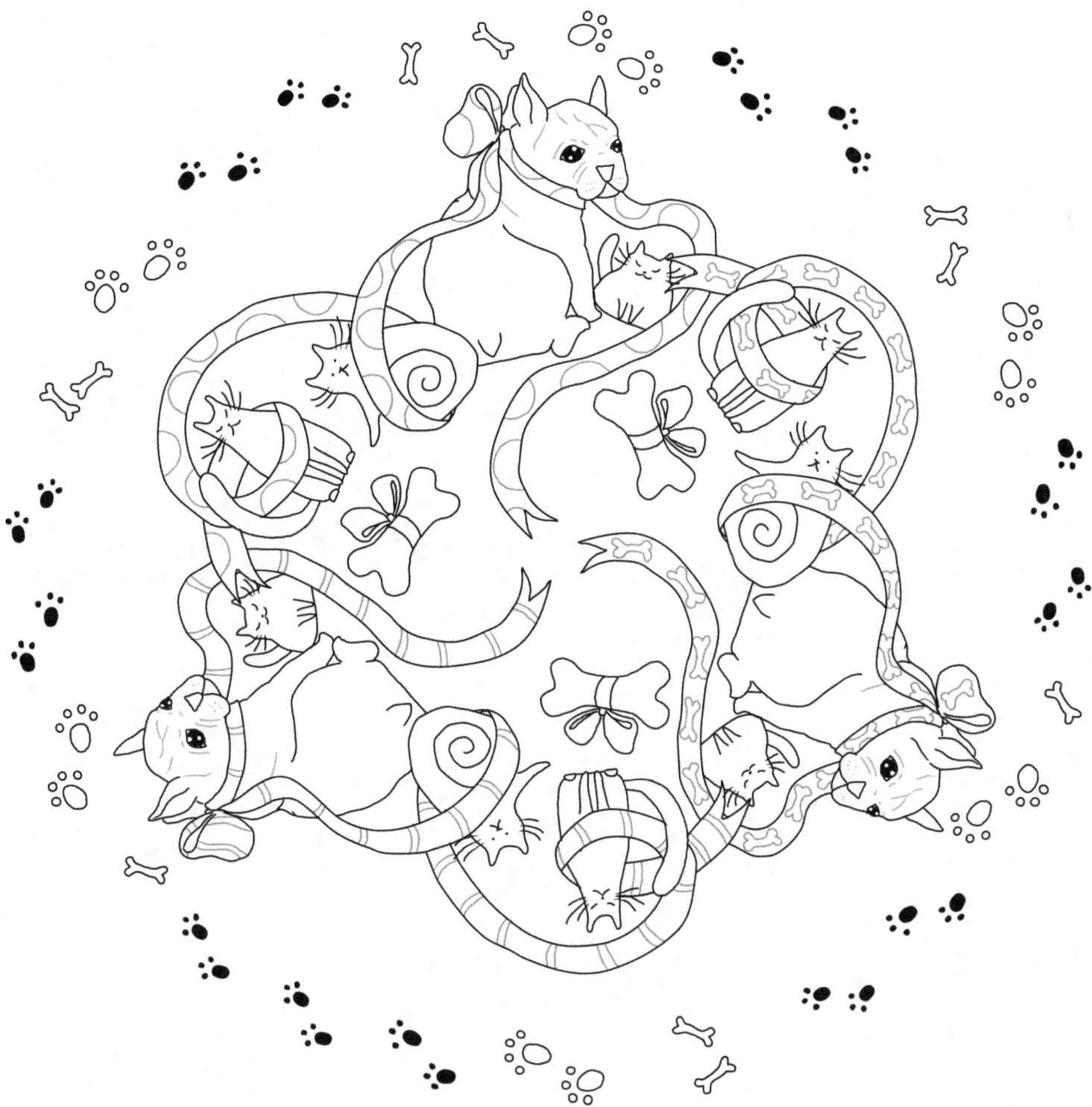

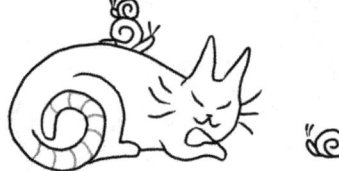

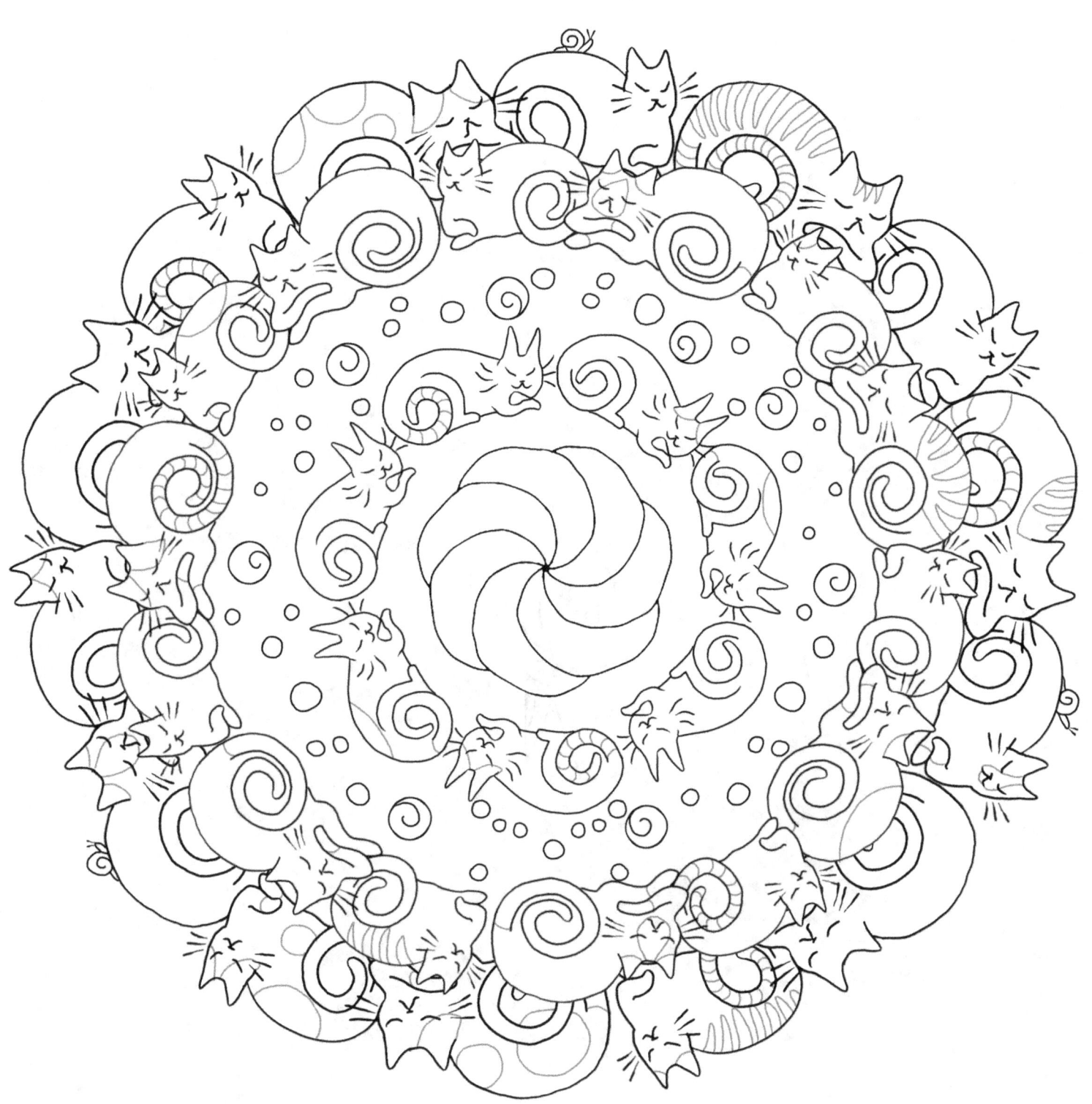

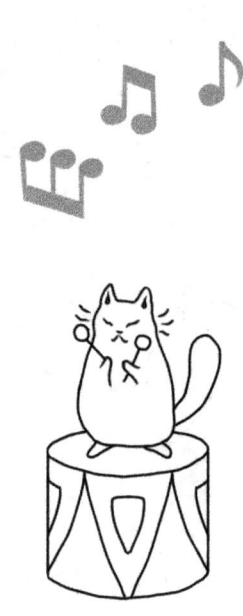

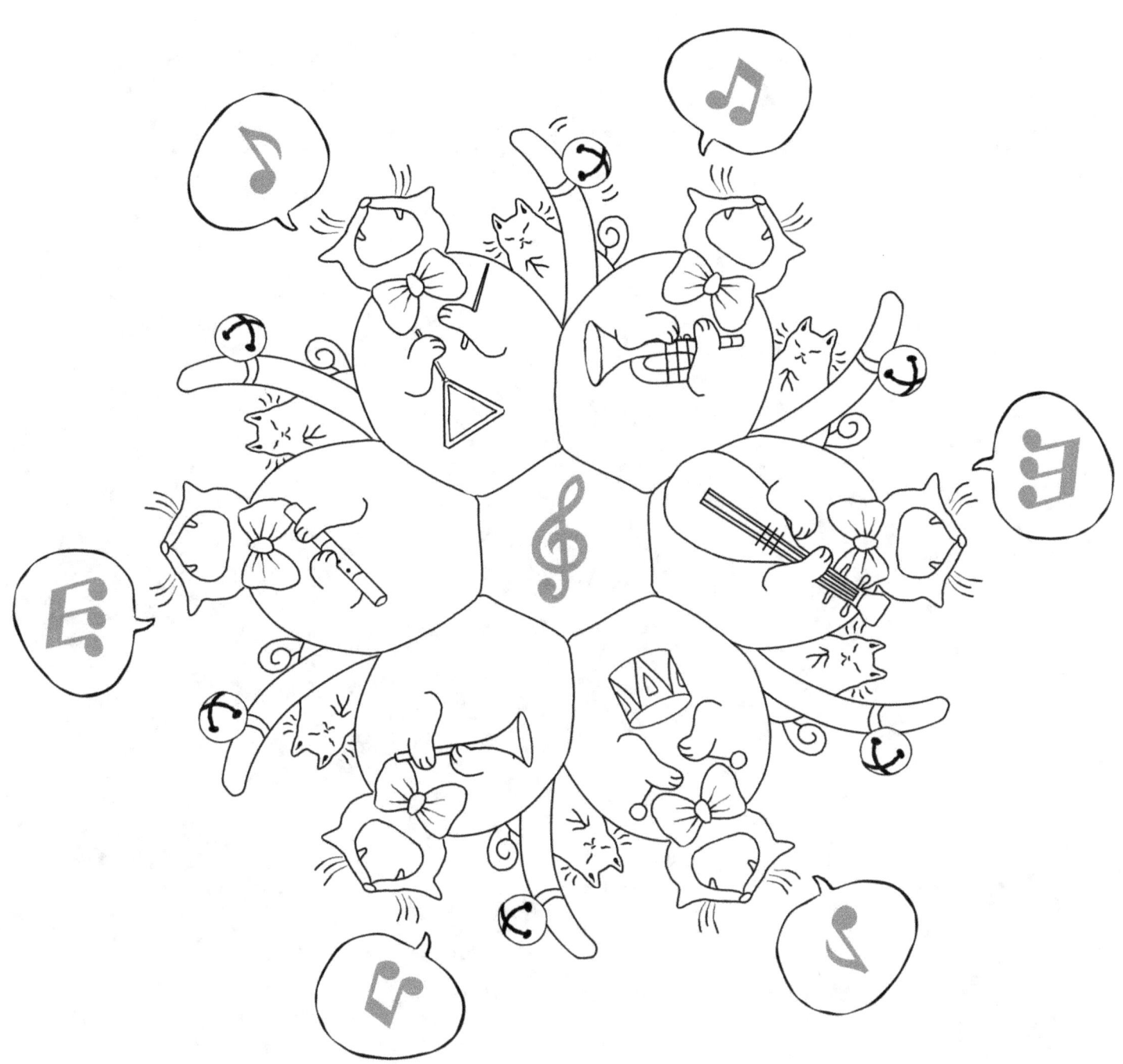

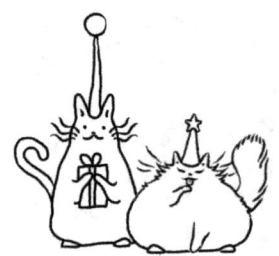

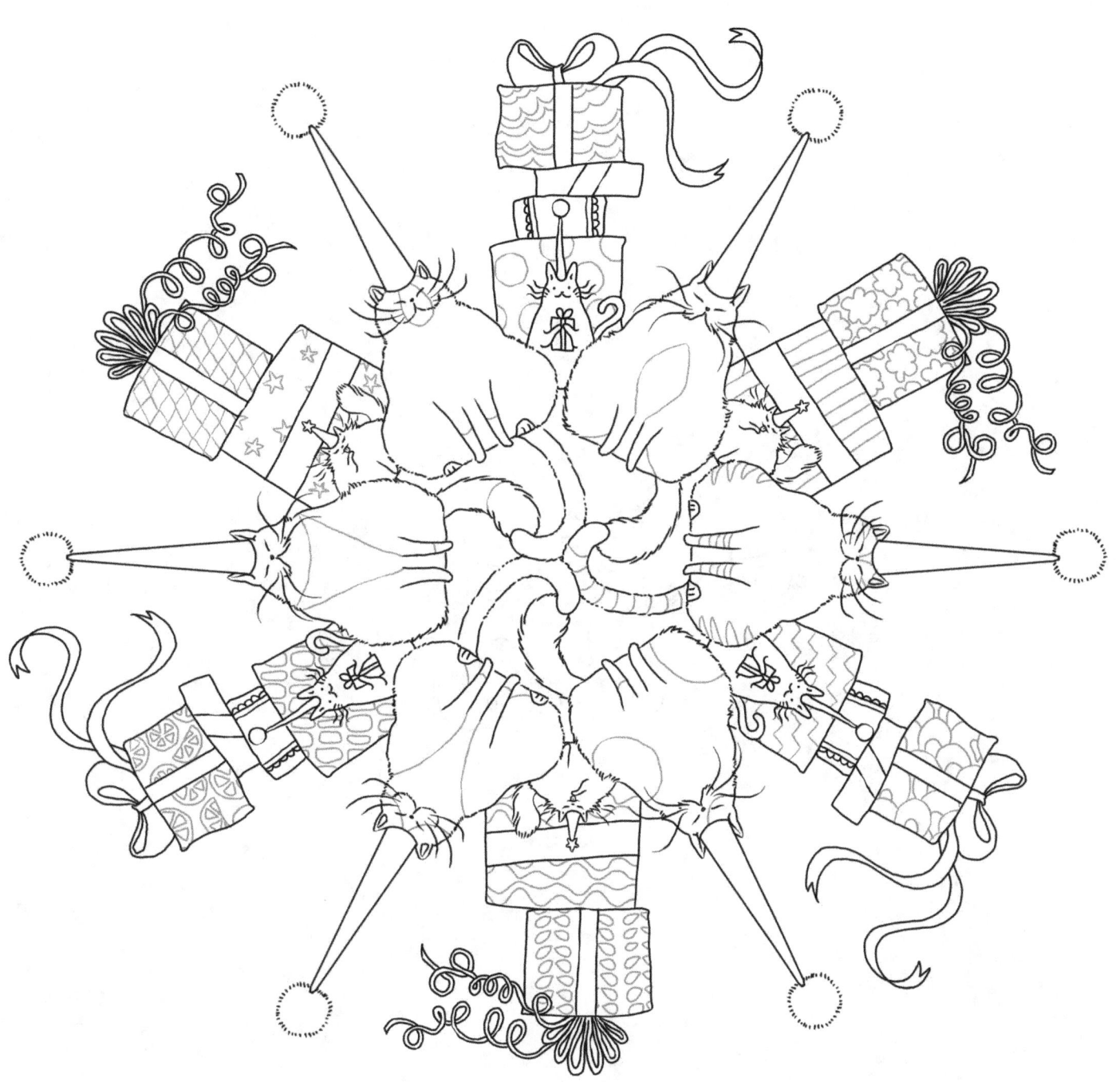

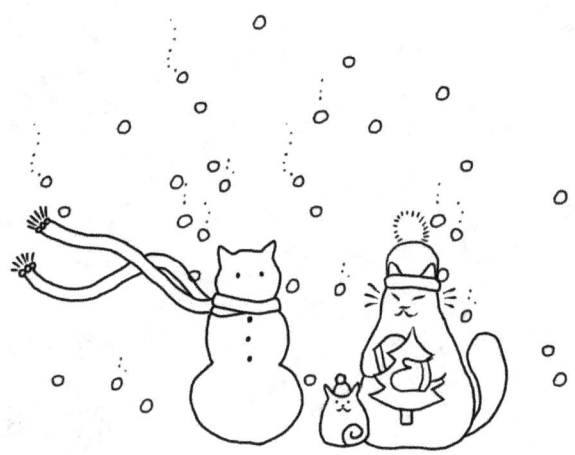

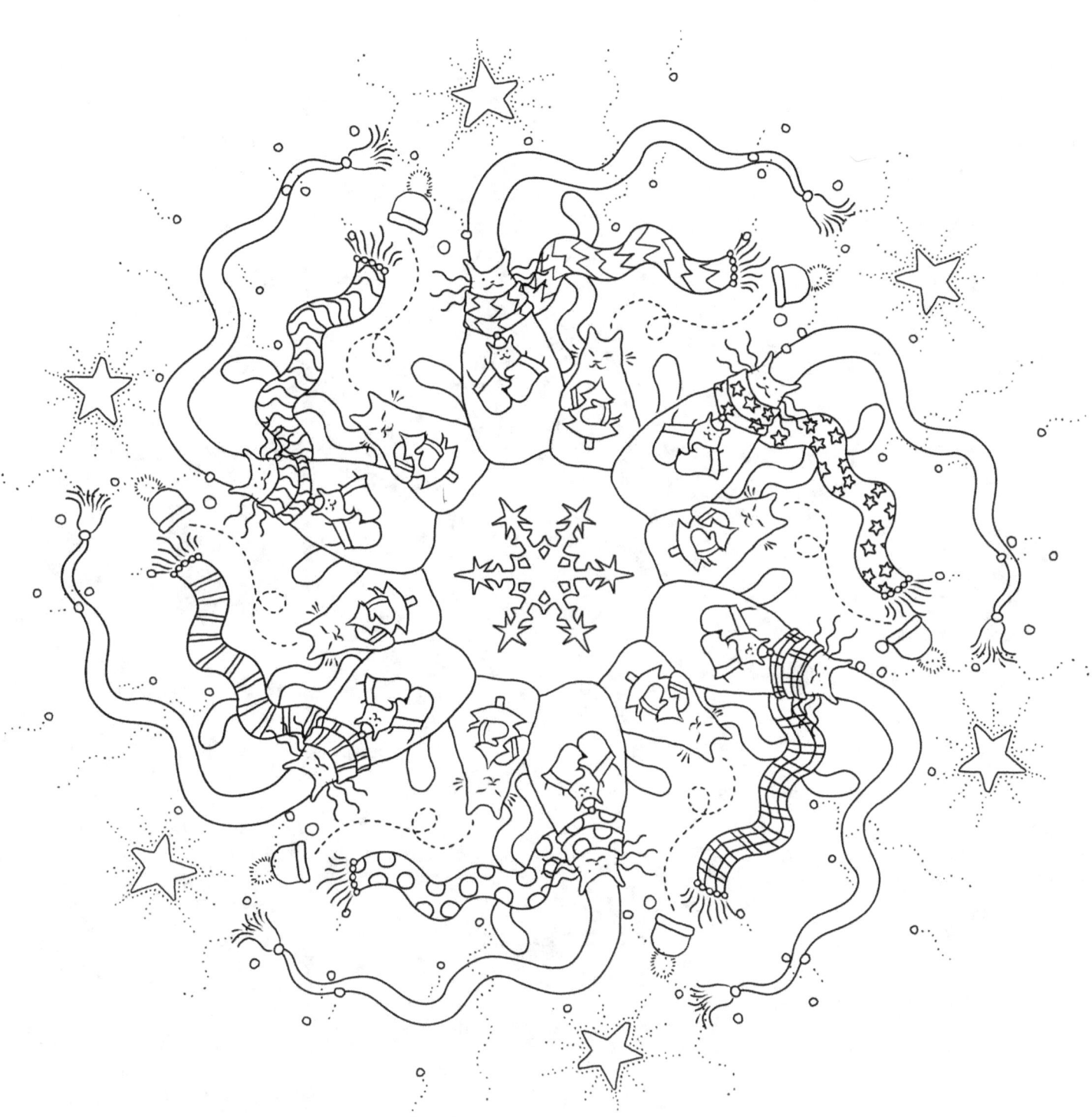

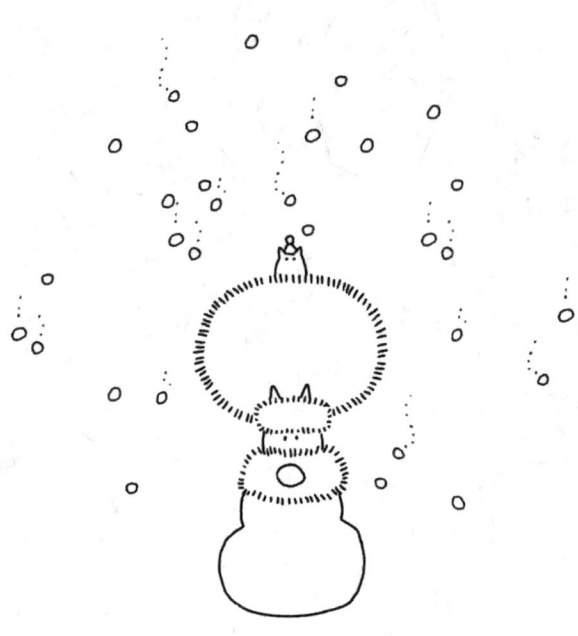

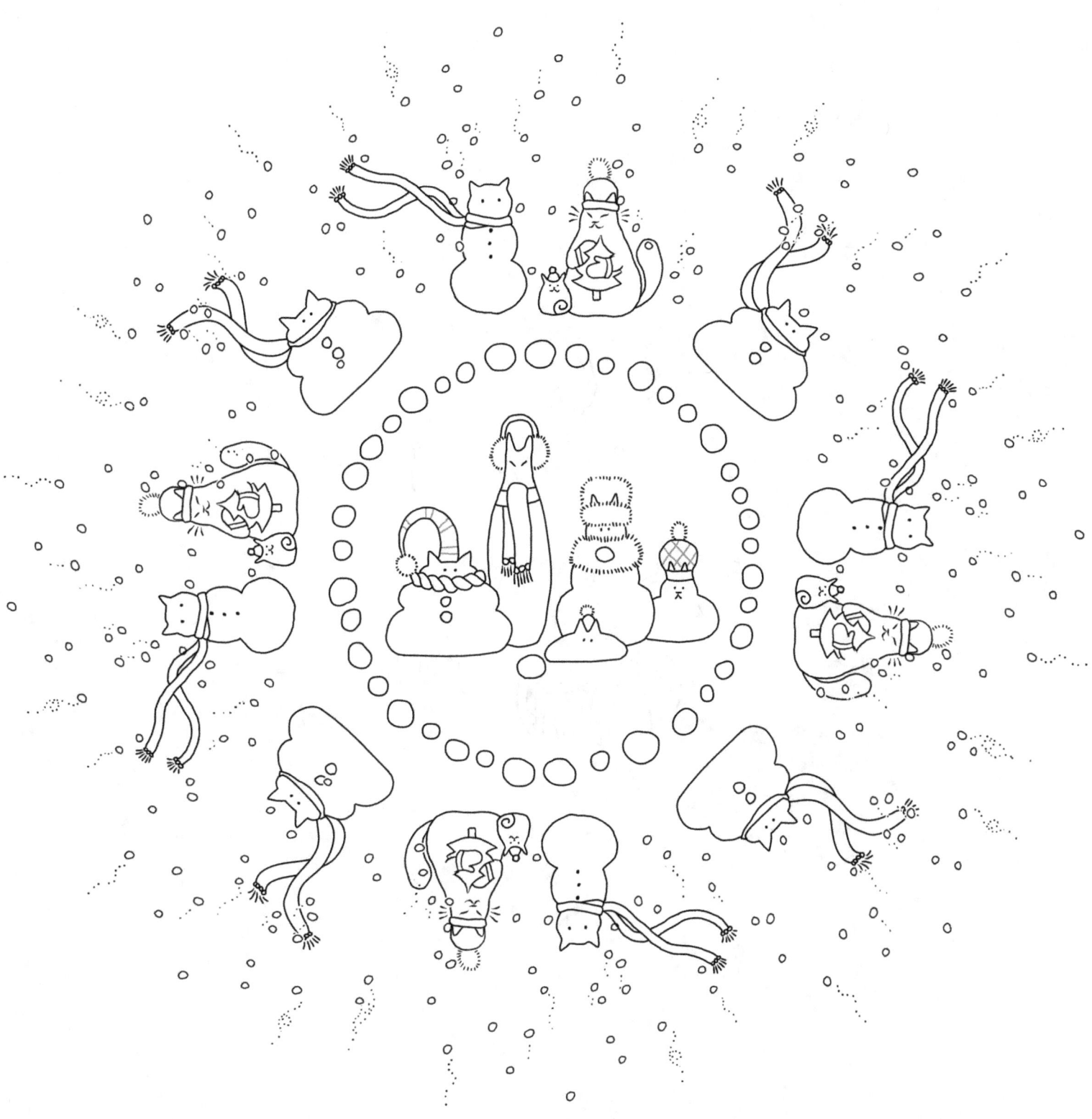

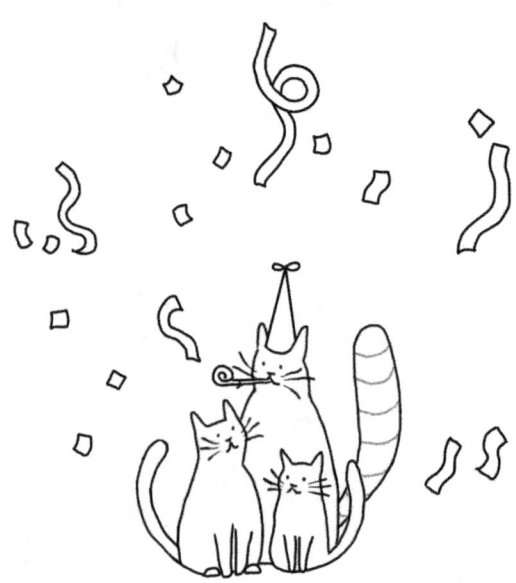

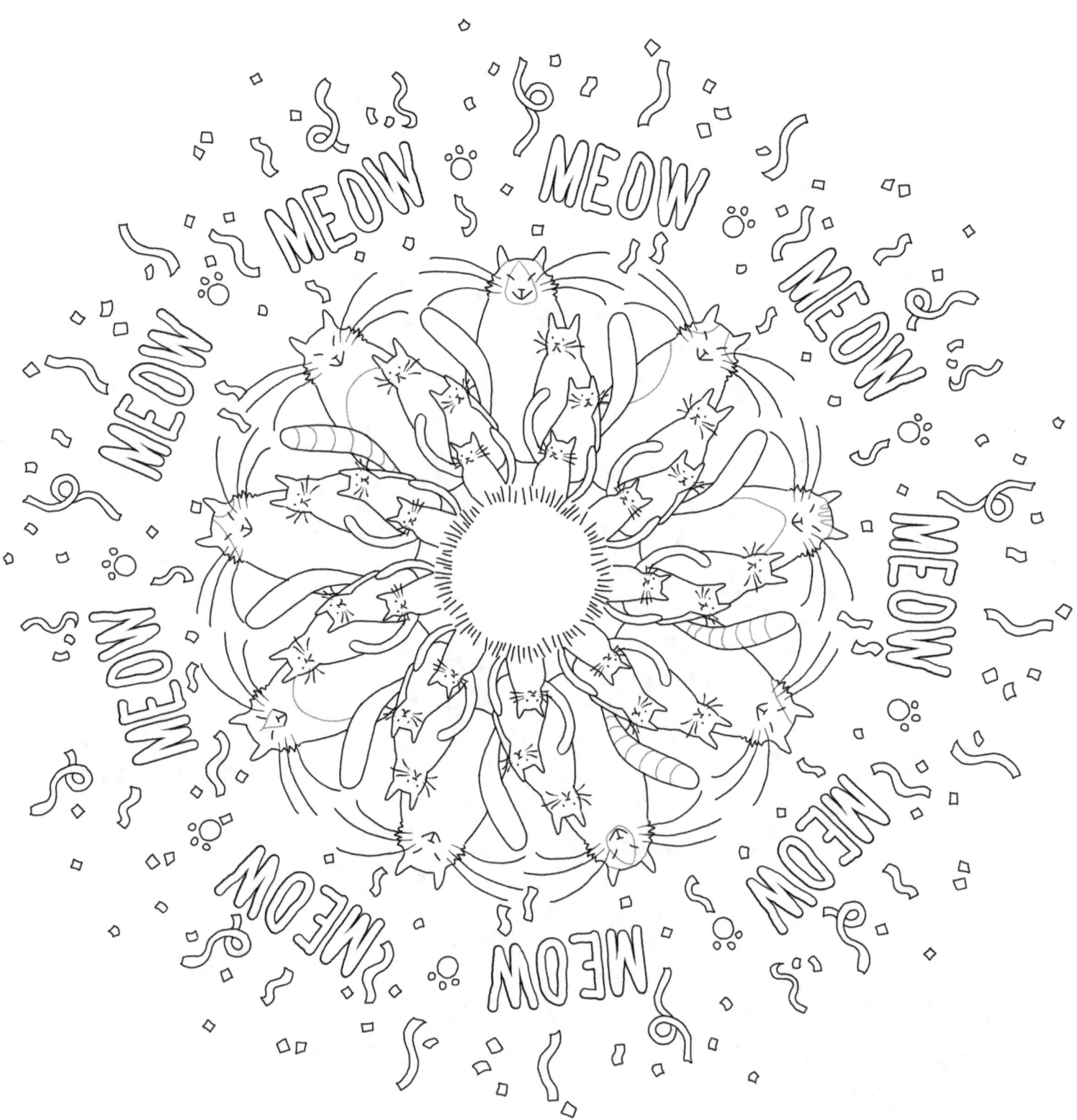

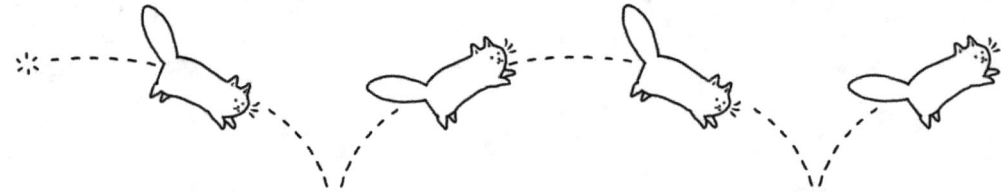

CONTACT THE PUBLISHER AND SEE
OTHER PUBLICATIONS AT
QUIXOTEPRESS.COM

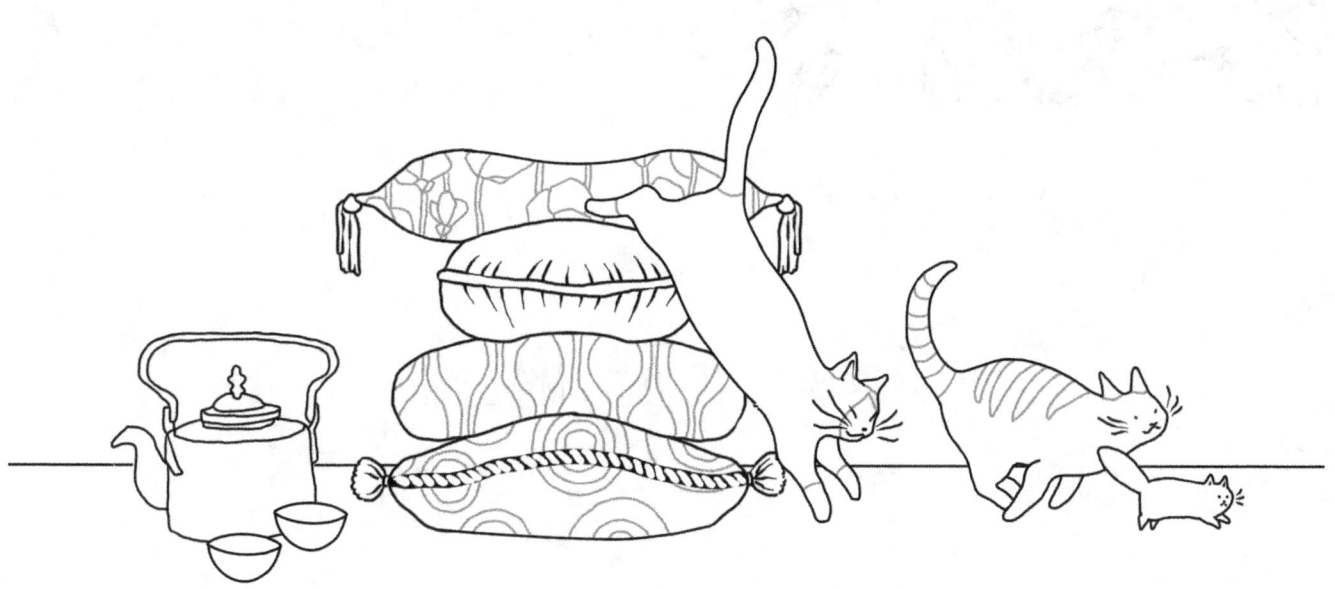

ALSO BY EVA CARRIERE:

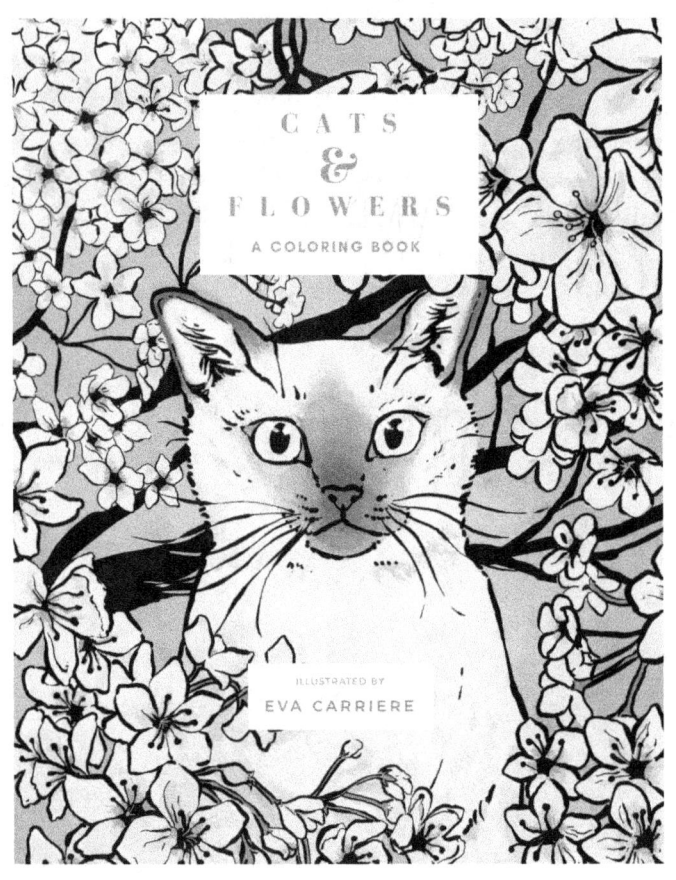

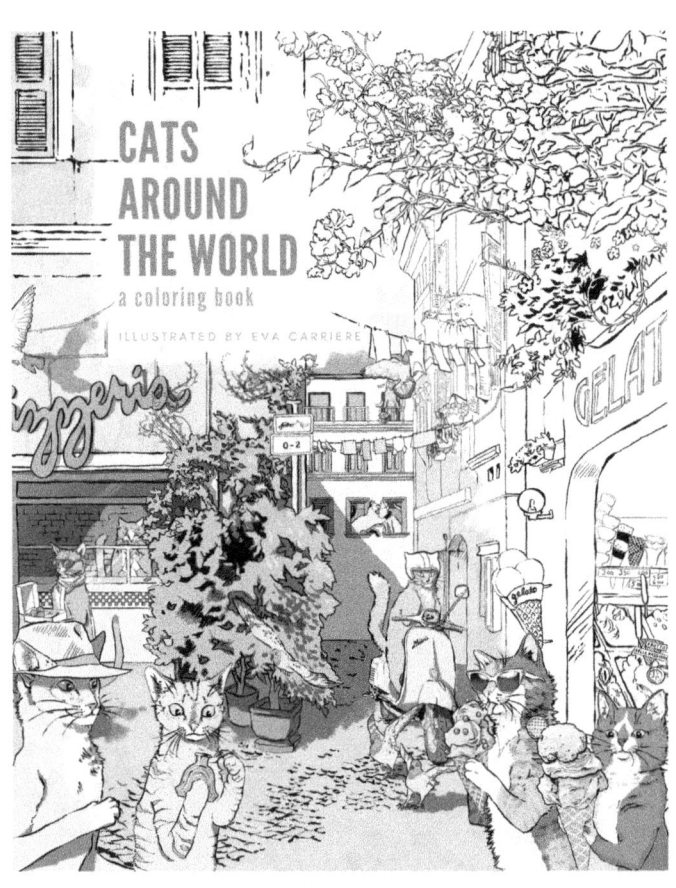

CATS & FLOWERS

CATS AROUND THE WORLD

AVAILABLE ON AMAZON!

 "The smallest feline is a masterpiece." —Leonardo da Vinci

www.ingramcontent.com/pod-product-compliance
Lightning Source LLC
Chambersburg PA
CBHW081249180526
45170CB00007B/2355